ISBN 978-1-330-13966-0
PIBN 10035457

English
Français
Deutsche
Italiano
Español
Português

www.forgottenbooks.com

Mythology Photography **Fiction**
Fishing Christianity **Art** Cooking
Essays Buddhism Freemasonry
Medicine **Biology** Music **Ancient
Egypt** Evolution Carpentry Physics
Dance Geology **Mathematics** Fitness
Shakespeare **Folklore** Yoga Marketing
Confidence Immortality Biographies
Poetry **Psychology** Witchcraft
Electronics Chemistry History **Law**
Accounting **Philosophy** Anthropology
Alchemy Drama Quantum Mechanics
Atheism Sexual Health **Ancient History**
Entrepreneurship Languages Sport
Paleontology Needlework Islam
Metaphysics Investment Archaeology
Parenting Statistics Criminology
Motivational

FISHERMEN'S WEATHER

A POOL ON THE TAY, DALGUISE

FISHERMEN'S WEATHER

BY UPWARDS OF ONE HUNDRED
LIVING ANGLERS

EDITED BY

F. G. AFLALO, F.R.G.S., F.Z.S.

EDITOR OF 'THE ENCYCLOPEDIA OF SPORT'
MEMBER OF COUNCIL OF THE SALMON AND TROUT ASSOCIATION
MEMBER OF THE MARINE BIOLOGICAL ASSOCIATION, ETC.

WITH EIGHT FULL-PAGE ILLUSTRATIONS IN COLOUR FROM

PAINTINGS BY CHARLES WHYMPER, F.Z.S.

LONDON
ADAM AND CHARLES BLACK
1906

EDITOR'S PREFACE

IN view of the meagre space allotted by the majority of angling writers[1] to considerations of wind and weather in their bearing on sport, an attempt has been made to obtain some expression of opinion, based on long and varied experience, from rather more than a hundred anglers of recognised qualifications for answering such an inquiry.

As the result of the uniform kindness with which my questions were answered, a mass of information, anecdote, and opinion soon became available, and this is

[1] Mr. W. Earl Hodgson's *Trout Fishing* and the second edition of Mr. Rolt's book on the grayling are notable exceptions to the general rule.

presented in the following chapters with some approach to logical order, a full index at the end facilitating cross-reference, so that any one can ascertain at a glance the most or least favourable weather conditions for any given fish in a number of well-known waters.

Throughout these pages the influence of weather on fishing is discussed solely in its relation to good or bad sport and without regard to the personal comfort of the sportsman. Of many such indirect results, however, the fisherman will always take account. He knows, for instance, that a wet day may keep a holiday crowd off the river or even away from its banks, and, being a selfish sportsman, he congratulates himself on such compensation for an otherwise uncomfortable day. This volume, however, has no concern with this aspect of the subject.

It is hoped that no one will suspect those responsible for the evidence collected

in these pages of any inclination to dogmatise, for they know far too much of
the uncertainties of fishing to make any
attempt at laying down the law as to
the effects of any atmospheric condition.

That our knowledge of this interesting
subject may "grow from more to more"
is both probable and desirable, yet, even
were infallible omniscience within our
grasp, we might be forgiven for declining
such a gift. On the day of perfect knowledge, when a glance at the aneroid
should tell the fisherman when it is
useless to leave his comfortable bed for
the dour river-side, such mechanical
prescience would rob the sport of half
its glamour.

All that has been attempted in these
pages is to collect a number of authentic
cases in which the contents' of the basket
have apparently been determined to a
great extent by certain conditions of

weather and temperature, together with some general statements of the best and worst wind and other conditions traditionally associated with a number of well-known rivers and lochs. In most cases, deduction has been left to the reader, who is thus free to exercise his own ingenuity in determining why, as the Jamaica niggers say: "Ebbry day good for fishing, but not ebbry day good for catch fish."

It remains only to thank those who have so kindly supplied the information asked for. Of its soundness, the names in the following list are sufficient guarantee.

	Reference Initials used in the Text.
Beale Adams, Esq., R.B.A. . .	B. A.
Richard Bagot, Esq. . . .	R. B.
Lieut.-Col. P. R. Bairnsfather .	P. R. B.
Dr. H. Brereton Baker, F.R.S. . .	H. B. B.
The Rev. W. Barker, M.A. (Rector of St. Marylebone)	W. B.
C. G. Barrington, Esq., C.B. . . .	C. G. B.
The late Canon St. Vincent Beechey .	St. V. B.
Dr. Joseph Bell, J.P., D.L. . . .	J. B.
John Bickerdyke	
A. W. Black, Esq., M.P. . . .	A. W. B.

	Reference Initials used in the Text.
Major C. P. Boulton, D.S.O. . . .	C. P. B.
The Rt. Hon. the Marquess of Breadalbane, K.G.	B.
The late Lady Bridge	H. M. F. B.
Dr. J. Franck Bright, D.D. .	J. F. B.
Colonel Archibald Broadfoot, C.B. . .	A. B.
Sir Douglas Brooke, Bt.	D. B.
The Rev. J. M. S. Brooke, M.A., F.R.G.S. (Rector of St. Mary, Woolnoth) .	J. M. S. B.
Sir George Thomas Brown, C.B. . .	G. T. B.
John Brown, Esq., F.R.S. . . .	J. Br.
H. A. Bryden, Esq. . .	H. A. B.
Sir R. H. W. Bulkeley, Bt. . .	R. H. W. B.
Prof. F. C. Burkitt, M.A., F.B.A. . .	F. C. B.
The Rt. Hon. Sydney Buxton, M.P. . .	S. B.
Colonel R. T. Caldwell, J.P., D.L. (Master of Corpus Christi College, Cambridge) .	R. T. C.
James Cantlie, Esq. . . .	J. C.
C. E. S. Chambers, Esq.	C. E. S. C.
Basil Champneys, Esq. .	B. C.
Dr. W. B. Cheadle .	W. B. C.
Dr. Charles Chree, F.R.S. .	C. C.
The Hon. Gilbert J. Coleridge	G. J. C.
Colonel C. G. Collingwood, C.B. . .	C. G. C.
Henry Daniel Conner, Esq., K.C., J.P. .	H. D. C.
Maj.-Gen. Arthur Domville Corbet, C.B. .	A. D. C.
Sir W. O. Dalgleish, Bt. .	W. O. D.
Maj.-Gen. James Cecil Dalton, R.A. .	J. C. D.
Colonel Bryan G. Davies-Cooke . .	B. G. D.-C.
The late Sir Clinton E. Dawkins, K.C.B.	C. E. D.
Prof. W. Boyd Dawkins, F.R.S. . .	W. B. D.
Colonel T. Deane, C.B. . .	T. D.
Lord Desborough	D.
G. Ashley Dodd, Esq. . . .	G. A. D.
Captain J. J. Dunne ("Hi Regan")	J. J. D.
Captain W. Edgworth-Johnstone .	W. E.-J.
C. E. Munro Edwards, Esq. . .	C. E. M. E.
Sir John Edwards-Moss, Bt. . .	J. E.-M.
Sir T. H. Grattan Esmonde, Bt., M.P.	T. H. G. E.

	Reference Initials used in the Text.
Major J. Wynn Eyton	J. W. E.
Sir J. D. Ferguson-Davie, Bt. . . .	J. D. F.-D.
The Rt. Hon. Sir James Fergusson, Bt. .	J. F.
Godfrey Fetherstonhaugh, Esq., K.C. . .	G. F.
The. Rev. Dr. Frederick Foakes-Jackson, D.D. (Dean of Jesus College, Cambridge)	F. F.-J.
William Warde Fowler, Esq., M.A. (Sub-Rector of Lincoln College, Oxford) .	W. W. F.
Walter M. Gallichan, Esq.	W. M. G.
The Hon. A. E. Gathorne-Hardy, J.P., D.L.	A. E. G.-H.
E. W. Gawthorne, Esq.	E. W. G.
Major H. C. Godley, D.S.O. . . .	H. C. G.
Lt.-Colonel H. H. Godwin-Austen, F.R.S. .	H. H. G.-A.
T. W. Gomm, Esq.	T. W. G.
A. M. Sutherland Graeme, Esq. . .	A. M. S. G.
The Rt. Hon. the Marquess of Granby .	G.
Hubert Hall, Esq.	H. H.
J. J. Hardy, Esq.	J. J. H.
J. A. Harvie-Brown, Esq. . . .	J. A. H.-B.
W. Earl Hodgson, Esq.	W. E. H.
Miss Rotha Hollins	R. H.
Horace Hutchinson, Esq. . . .	H. H.
Admiral Sir W. R. Kennedy, K.C.B. . .	W. R. K.
Sir Roper Lethbridge, K.C.I.E., K.B. . .	R. L.
Colonel Charles M'Inroy, C.B., J.P., D.L.	C. M'I.
Colonel E. D. Malcolm of Poltalloch, C.B. .	E. D. M.
R. B. Marston, Esq. (Editor of the *Fishing Gazette*)	R. B. M.
The Rev. W. A. Mathews, M.A. (Rector of Bassingham)	W. A. M.
A. R. Matthews, Esq. (Editor, *The Angler's News*)	A. R. M.
The Rt. Hon. Sir Herbert E. Maxwell, Bt., F.R.S.	H. E. M.
Harold Michelmore, Esq. . . .	H. M.
C. O. Minchin, Esq. . .	C. O. M.
Lord Montagu of Beaulieu . .	M.
Sir Samuel Montagu, Bt., J.P., D.L. . .	S. M.
Colonel R. St. Leger Moore, C.B., J.P.	R. St. L. M.

Reference Initials
used in the Text.

J. Lloyd Morgan, Esq., M.P. . . .	J. L. M.
Maj.-Gen. Sir Gerald de Courcy Morton, K.C.I.E., C.B., C.V.O.	G. de C. M.
Dr. George Murray . . .	G. M.
Dr. William Murray . . .	W. M.
Robert Noble, Esq., R.S.A.	R. N.
The Rt. Hon. Sir Ford North, P.C., F.R.S.	F. N.
Maj.-Gen. Desmond O'Callaghan, C.V.O., R.A.	D. O'C.
The Hon. F. Standish O'Grady . .	F. S. O'G.
Sir Henry Pottinger, Bt. . . .	H. P.
Sir Colman Battie Rashleigh, Bt.	C. B. R.
H. A. Rolt, Esq.	H. A. R.
Maj.-Gen. J. C. Russell, C.V.O. . .	J. C. R.
William Russell, Esq.	W. R.
W. Dendy Sadler, Esq.	W. D. S.
William Senior, Esq. (Editor of *The Field*) .	W. S.
Sir Henry Seton-Karr, C.M.G., J.P., D.L. .	H. S.-K.
A. Marmaduke Sheild, Esq., F.R.C.S. . .	A. M. S.
H. T. Sheringham, Esq. (Angling Editor of *The Field*)	H. T. S.
J. E. Smart, Esq.	J. E. S.
Colonel A. J. Stead	A. J. S.
The Rt. Hon. the Earl of Suffolk and Berkshire	S.
The Bishop Suffragan of Swansea . .	Sw.
Maj.-Gen. Sir Alexander B. Tulloch, K.C.B.	A. B. T.
John S. Tulloch, Esq.	J. S. T.
Colonel William Cornwallis West, J.P., C.C. (Lord-Lieutenant of Denbighshire) .	W. C. W.
C. H. Wheeley, Esq.	C. H. W.
Lord Wolverton	W.

It is with deep regret that I draw attention to the death of three valued contributors, the late Canon Beechey, the late Lady Bridge, and the late Sir Clinton Dawkins, while this book was in preparation.

Though such a course is opposed to the original plan of the work, it has been thought desirable to retain the notes which they so kindly sent.

F. G. A.

Teignmouth,
Easter 1906.

CONTENTS

PAGE

INTRODUCTION . 1

CHAPTER I

SUNSHINE 64

CHAPTER II

OF RAIN AND INCIDENTALLY OF HAIL AND
SLEET 102

CHAPTER III

OF FROST AND SNOW 140

CHAPTER IV

OF WIND . 164

CHAPTER V

OF THUNDER AND LIGHTNING . . 205

xiii

CHAPTER VI

PAGE

OF FOG AND MIST 228

APPENDIX

BEST AND WORST WEATHER (SPRING AND AUTUMN)
FOR CERTAIN WATERS 244

INDEX 248

LIST OF ILLUSTRATIONS

IN COLOUR

From Pictures by CHARLES WHYMPER, F.Z.S.

A POOL ON THE TAY, DALGUISE . . *Frontispiece*

ON THE AVON, HANTS . *Facing page* 14

A SMALL BUT GOOD POOL „ 84

SALMON JUMPING THE FALLS . „ 126

A ROUGH DAY AND BOILING WATER „ 154

CASTING INTO AN AWKWARD CORNER „ 190

LOCH TROOL . . . „ 214

"CHANGING THE FLY" . „ 242

FISHERMEN'S WEATHER

INTRODUCTION

Weather as an excuse for failure—Weather in other
sports—Cases in which the influence of weather is
negligible—Mr. Hutchinson's views—Importance of
body of water in the river—Salmon, sea-trout, and
Thames trout insensible to weather and temperature
—Brown trout taken in all weathers—Educated trout
more susceptible to weather than others—Mr. W. Earl
Hodgson on symptoms—Earthquakes—What is ideal
fishing weather?—Cold-weather fish—Concealing
the fraud—No consensus of expert opinion regarding
weather—Colonel Bairnsfather's "normal weather"
theory—Mr. Harvie-Brown on the deterioration of
the British climate—The spring of 1905—Mr. Munro
Edwards on the same subject—Weather lore in fishes
—The late Matthias Dunn's theory—Norfolk trout at
fault: Mr. Hall's experience—Sunshine—Is rising
short due to light?—Possible effect of solar eclipse
—Fish dazzled by sunshine—Rain and hail—Frost and
snow—Cases of good sport in "snow-broth"—Wind—
Thunder and lightning—Fog and mist—What, then,
is bad fishing weather?—Other conditions besides
those enumerated—Weather and sea-fishing—John
Bickerdyke's views—The moral of this book.

THE fisherman's first impulse, on getting
out of bed on a holiday morning, is to

pull up the blind and look at the sky. An aneroid barometer knows more of the coming weather than the sky, yet both are untrustworthy so far as the mood of the fish is concerned; and the best plan, unless the day is actually too bad for enjoyment, is to take no notice of the weather, but to get to the waterside as soon as possible and there tempt fortune.

At the same time, even though, in the light of past experience or in obedience to the warnings of those who know, we refuse to let the sky signs move us to either unwarranted optimism or unnecessary despair, it cannot fail to be of interest to determine such conditions of light or temperature, such manifestations of electrical disturbance, such changes in the quality or quantity of the wind as appear to exercise an appreciable, though not a constant, influence on the sport of fishing with rod and line.

To attach, therefore, a due and not exaggerated significance to the part played by atmospheric conditions in the day's bag is not necessarily to go to the other extreme, and invariably tax the weather with the responsibility for an empty creel, which should rather have been attributed to bad fishing. Failure invariably seeks an impersonal excuse, usually summed up in the somewhat vague expression "bad luck," and the weather is, in the course of such explanation, apt to come in for more than its share of the blame. Success, though quite as likely to be due to similar causes, is rarely accounted for on such grounds. Yet there is no weather, indeed no art, so bad as invariably to produce a blank day. Success, as unexpected as it is delightful, is always possible by reason of the caprice of the fish.

The significance of weather is not the same in all outdoor sports. Frost means more to the hunting man than to those who fish or shoot. Rain may easily ruin a day's shooting, making the birds fly badly and spoiling them for table purposes when picked up. A pastime like

skating is obviously, in the open air at
any rate, possible only in a certain
condition of temperature, while yachting
is equally dependent on the prevalence
of wind.   Fishing, while never perhaps
wholly arrested by any condition except
drought, is more susceptible than most
sports to those shades of difference, on
which the favourable conditions directly
depend : the level and colour of the river
on the rainfall; the hatch of fly on the
temperature ; the success, or even the
possibility, of fly-fishing on the strength
and direction of the wind.

Cases in
which the
influence of
weather is
negligible.

It is apparent from much of the
correspondence on which these chapters
are based that many anglers of wide and
varied experience regard the influence of
weather conditions as sometimes, though
by no means always, negligible.   Some
have found that its effect is insignificant
in the case of certain rivers and lakes,
while others discount its importance in
the case only of a particular species of
fish.   As a case of the former, reference

may be made to the River Eden, at Armathwaite, of which Dr. William Murray writes in the following terms: "I can catch a good basket in almost any weather, both when the river is high and when dead low, and on bright, cloudless days. Under the latter conditions, I get them under the trees and in the open, basking on the flat rocks, which run well out into the river. . . . For my part, I do not think that any rules as to weather have a general application. What suits one place does not suit another. I have done very well in the most boisterous, bitter weather in April or September, and have returned with an empty creel after a warm, dull day, with slightly coloured water and everything favourable. Truly, the ways of trout are past finding out by the wit of man."

"It is," writes Admiral Sir Michael Culme Seymour, "within the experience of most anglers that they have caught fish in every possible sort of weather." Another fisherman of forty-five years' experience, Colonel St. Leger Moore, admits that he has lived to see the failure of almost every rule and theory regarding the relations between fishing and the weather inculcated in his boyhood. The Rev. J. M. S. Brooke attaches no importance whatever to any meteorological conditions, except perhaps the absence of all ripple from the water, or a very brilliant sun. Fish, he thinks, are all eye and no ear, and so long as they are on the feed, weather should not appreciably interfere with the chances of any one who can throw a useful fly.

Mr. Standish O'Grady considers that no fisherman can prognosticate results by weather conditions. "I hold," he adds, "that it is quite possible to do well with salmon on the brightest days, but I doubt whether one can have too much wind."

Mr. Hutchinson's views.

Mr. Horace Hutchinson holds a somewhat similar opinion on the same subject. "I think," he writes, "that a great deal too much is made of the influence of weather on fish from the angler's point of

view. There are only two features of the
atmosphere that, in my opinion, are fatal
to success with trout, and, in less degree,
with salmon : the one is a mist, coming
down thick and low on the river; the
other is the appearance of bright, white,
hummocky clouds in a clear sky. People
tell you a lot about fish coming short in
consequence of the angle of light on the
water. This, I think, is all very specu-
lative. Again, when they tell you that
fish rise directly after the rain begins and
stop as soon as it leaves off, I think that
this really means that when the drops
were falling, the surface was broken by
them, and the lure was therefore able to
delude the fish as it could not when the
surface was calm. Wind, of course, acts
in the same way, more obviously in loch-
fishing. In a ripple, you will catch fish
at every cast, but when it dies down, you
will not catch one. If the water is low,
you will not catch fish with a bright, clear
sky, but again it is all a question of the
fish seeing the lure too plainly. Naturally,

the indirect effects of weather, in altering the height and colour of the water, have an immense influence, but the immediate effect of changes is either nil, or else so subtle in its cause that we cannot understand it.   That, at least, is my opinion."

Importance of body of water in the river.

General Tulloch, who has had a long experience of renting stretches on the Usk, the Ristagouche (Canada), a Norwegian river, and some fishing on the Ness (during a tenancy of two years on the last he kept faithful day and night registers of the temperature), considers that the run of salmon depends wholly on the body of water in the river and not in the least on weather conditions.   Nor is he alone in regarding the body of water as of much greater importance than either weather or temperature.   Mr. Conner writes of the Bandon River : "The best day is immediately after the rise of the river after rain is over.   You will then kill salmon in practically any weather."   Again: "In every river that I have fished," says Sir Henry Seton-Karr, "(and they are many), the experienced local fishermen know, to an inch almost, the proper height for every throw."

It would seem as if the larger game fish, salmon, sea-trout and Thames trout were all at certain times, and in some waters at any rate, insensible to the influence of weather and temperature.

Of the first, Sir Herbert Maxwell writes: "Given no excess of sunshine, I have yet to learn what is a bad day for salmon fishing. If fish are in the water, some are sure to be on the move, but, as they are not feeding, naturally they are more capricious than trout." As regards the connection between salmon fishing and temperature, Sir Henry Seton-Karr writes: "Anglers break the ice on the Thurso in January, and on Deeside in February; they shake the ice from line and rod-rings on the Tweed in November, and in all these cases catch salmon freely on the fly; while on summer evenings many an Irish and Norwegian salmon-river yield their best sport." Dr. Bright

Salmon, sea-trout, and Thames trou insensible to weather and temperature.

lays similar stress on the extreme latitude in the matter of weather and temperature accorded to the salmon-fisherman. "I have," he says, "found salmon taking eagerly in the most glaring sun, when the hollows of the wavelets were deep blue and the crests so brilliant a silver that you could scarcely look at them. I have taken fish equally well on sullen, dark, thundery days, when the water was all brown and grey. I have taken them when it was so cold that the line threatened to freeze, and, again, when so hot that the metal of the rod was unpleasant to touch, but scarcely ever without a breeze. I believe that the movement of the water, possibly its increased oxidation, is the real thing affecting fish. I do not think it is because the ripple hides the hook." The last sentence in Dr. Bright's interesting summary is in bold conflict with the almost universally accepted opinion that a ripple is necessary, especially in the still water of lakes, to hide the glint of the gut; but this is more appropriately discussed on a later page.

Of sea-trout, Lord Montagu of Beaulieu writes: "I have caught them in all kinds of weather—rainstorms, hailstorms, thunderstorms, etc., and in bright weather with an east wind." Nor are the experiences of Mr. Wheeley with Thames trout, with which he has had great success, less varied, since of those fish he has "killed one in a blinding snowstorm and others in blazing sun and clear water." These catches under conditions so varied have led him to conclude that the Thames trout may be killed "in all conditions of water and weather, raging flood or summer drought."

In some waters, at any rate, it looks as if brown trout are scarcely more affected by weather and temperature than their bigger relatives, though their appetites are necessarily affected by either a rise in temperature, which may bring out a hatch of fly, or a shower of rain, which may wash down a harvest of worms.

Brown trout taken in all weathers.

" I suppose," writes Sir Herbert Maxwell, " that the rising of trout takes place when, and only when, larvæ are rising simultaneously to the surface to become flies. Of course, a casual trout will rise at stray flies blown into the water; and in shallow northern streams, where small trout are hungry, they are on the lookout for flies, or any other form of food, at almost all times and in all weathers. But the regular rise is dependent on the rise of fly, and that, of some species, seems to depend on *season and hour of day*, irrespective of weather. For instance, one March, on a bitter, blustery day, with driving snow and the river full of floating and fixed ice, there was a tremendous rise of March Browns on the Helmsdale, which the trout were ravenously devouring, though the water temperature was only 33° F. No angler would have found any encouragement from the text-books to go forth under such a sky. Yet he might have filled a big basket. The biggest rise of March Browns I ever

saw was on the Tay in April (1905):
weather bitter, with hard north wind.
The river was alive with rising trout,
but, as usual, I was after salmon. It is
the same in lakes. I have had good and
fast sport with strong east wind in spring.
Sometimes, on such a day, a heavy snowstorm brings up the fly and the trout
after them. I recollect especially one
morning when there was a big rise of
duns. I could hardly see to cast for
snowflakes, but I caught big trout very
quickly. Contrariwise, in lochs especially, the most promising weather and
water may also be a fraud. All depends
whether flies happen to be coming up."

Mr. Michelmore, who has had long
experience of the moorland trout-streams
of Devonshire, has made good baskets on
the Exe during a thunderstorm, on the
Teign during a snowstorm, on the Barle
during a hailstorm, and on the Coley
when the water was so thick from previous
rain that it seemed impossible for trout to
see the fly.

Educated
trout more
susceptible to
weather than
others.

If one rule seems more reasonable than others, it is that educated trout in much-fished waters are far more sensitive to weather influences than those which know little of the ways of man. It will not escape notice in the following chapters that the fish of the Thames, Tweed, Tay, and other much-flogged waters are far more influenced by weather than those of more isolated districts. Major Boulton mentions a case of the close relations that exist between fishing and the weather in the island of North Uist, the highly educated trout of which are peculiarly susceptible to such influences, while Colonel Cornwallis West contrasts the educated trout of Hampshire chalk-streams with the unsophisticated fish of Welsh rivers, and points out that the latter are little affected by the weather. The comparative insensibility of unedu-cated trout to changes of the weather is also noted by Sir Henry Seton-Karr, who, during his experiences in the Western States of America, had exceptional oppor-

ON THE AVON, HANTS

tunities of contrasting the simple fish of rivers new to the fly-fisherman with those of more frequented waters at home. "The best brown trout," he writes, "of the Irish Erne—and these run up to 8 lbs. weight and even more—are hardly ever caught, except at night, when we must presume that they cannot see the line. By the kindness of the proprietors, the trout fishing on the Erne is free, and the trout in consequence much fished over and highly educated. On the other hand, it has been my lot to enjoy some excellent trout fishing in the heart of the Rockies, in the clear mountain-streams that drain the western watershed of Northern Wyoming. I doubt if the trout in those streams had then ever seen an artificial fly before, and so I had an opportunity of studying the primitive ways of trout absolutely ignorant of the wiles of the angler. Their eagerness and voracity for almost any size or colour of fly, within reason, was delightful, and, as they ran up to 4 lbs. weight, they afforded much sport, besides welcome food for a hungry camp. The only weather condition that seriously affected the rise was, so far as my experience and observation went, the temperature. The brighter and hotter the sun, the more lively and voracious as a rule were the trout. When the cool of the evening came on, particularly in September, the rise usually ceased."

Mr. W. Earl Hodgson on symptoms.

From these evidences, with others to be adduced in subsequent chapters, it is obvious that hard and fast rules are foreign to the subject of the present inquiry, and these instances have been cited at the outset with a view to laying stress on the absence of dogma from this attempt to review our present knowledge of the meaning of weather and temperature to the fisherman. Indeed Mr. W. Earl Hodgson, whose charming work on *Trout Fishing* has already been mentioned as devoting exceptional attention to the subject of the weather, is of opinion that not one of the conditions which give their names to the following chapters is actually responsible for good or bad sport, but that each may be symptomatic of some more or less complex set of conditions not without influence on the appetite of the fish.   This interesting suggestion opens up a wider scope of inquiry than that planned for the present volume, and is quoted only for the benefit of such contemplative anglers as may care in their leisure to follow it up.

Another most interesting hypothesis, Earthquakes suggested by Mr. Sheringham, must also be dismissed with passing notice, chiefly for want of sufficient data.   Mr. Sheringham's view is that periods of European earthquake have been synchronous with poor fishing results.   This suggestion, which may perhaps be borne out by the experience of others, may prove that the influence of even remote seismic disturbance can make itself felt on a class of animals that, outside the area of actual upheaval, would seem peculiarly immune from its effects.

What is
ideal fishing
weather?

As distinct from a purely academic interest inseparable from such inquiries, the strictly practical use of such evidence as has been collected in the present volume is to acquaint the fisherman with the best and worst weather for his sport with particular fish and in waters of well-marked climatic conditions. Much depends on what individual sportsmen expect of the weather. The mere consideration of personal comfort, the objection to rain, the aversion from frost or east wind, or the fear of lightning, are not without their bearing on this diversity of opinion, but are, as has been explained, outside the scope of these chapters. Something, however, of the view as to what constitutes ideal fishing weather depends on the part which the weather is supposed to play in the day's sport. Briefly, favourable weather may accomplish two purposes: it may make the fish eager to feed, and it may help to conceal the deceptions practised by the fisherman. The first would seem to be a matter mainly of temperature; the second, mainly one of light. A high temperature is as a rule the one which makes trout feed by bringing up a hatch of fly, yet so experienced a dry-fly fisherman as Mr. Sydney Buxton has observed that a cold day sometimes produces the heaviest and strongest hatch, so that, even in the choice of temperature, tastes will vary in accordance with individual experience. A low temperature may indirectly enhance the value of the fisherman's bait in another manner, by either killing or driving elsewhere the natural food of the fish. A case in point is mentioned by Mr. Wheeley, who attributes much of his success with Thames trout in weirs during a bitter spell of east wind to the cold having driven the bleak out of such spots, and consequently leaving the famished trout ravenous for the bleak used by the angler as bait.

With regard to those fish which do not depend for their food on a hatch of fly, it is a matter of opinion whether they feed better in a high or low temperature. A

Cold-weather fish.

very few, like the barbel, are apparently only rarely caught during the winter months, and roach appear to feed best in frosty weather in some waters, while in others, under the same conditions, they seem to fast.

Concealing the fraud.

Dr. Bright's opinion that the ripple on the water, which the majority of fly-fishermen prefer even in rivers, and in lake-fishing find indispensable, is of no service in concealing the gut cast, has already been referred to. It may be the correct one, but it is fair to say that it is opposed to the opinion current among fishermen. The extent to which a strong or moderate light, or a ruffling breeze on the surface, may hide the fisherman's tackle cannot be precisely determined, since such an esti-mate would entail accurate knowledge of how an object like an artificial fly appears to the eye of the fish. Even the range of vision in fishes is not known with any certainty, though even so highly organised a fish as a salmon is said to see an object under water no more than six inches away. We are, however, for practical purposes concerned rather with how fishes see an object dropped on the surface of the water, between their eye, that is to say, and the source of all natural light. This may be a very different matter, and some measure of concealment is presumably afforded by either of the extreme conditions of an overcast sky or a dazzling sun. The vision of the fish may, that is, be equally handicapped by too little or too much light. For this reason, there is an old-fashioned prejudice in favour of a dark fly for bright days and a bright one for dull weather, but the practical application of this rule is subject to many exceptions. The portion of his tackle which most betrays the wiles of the fisherman is his gut, the apparently indestructible glint of which must always be fatal to perfect concealment. Beside the conspicuous apparition of the gut, the mere colour of the fly, as seen against a well-lighted background, may, though its size be all-important, amount to a negligible quantity.

No consensus
of expert
opinion
regarding
weather.

From even the foregoing selection of divergent opinion as to the influence of typical conditions of light, weather, and temperature, the absence of any stereotyped ideal weather to suit all tastes, fish, and rivers will at once be apparent. From the whole of the following pages, indeed, it would in all probability be impossible to select a single condition, or set of conditions, on which, even among the comparatively few fishermen who have been good enough to contribute the material, there is unanimity of friendly or adverse opinion.

Colonel
Bairnsfather's
"normal
weather"
theory.

The view that different weather suits different localities finds general expression in what Colonel Bairnsfather, a fisherman of lifelong experience in both this country and India, calls his "normal weather" theory. Briefly, the meaning of this is that he regards the normal weather of India as most favourable for catching mahseer, and the normal weather of Great Britain as most suitable for catching trout. The latter fish, as he points out, are often shy on the brightest days ; on the other hand, it is in clear, bright weather that the best mahseer are caught. General Morton shares this opinion of the best mahseer weather, though Colonel Deane adds that on these bright days he never made a good bag of mahseer, unless there was also a breeze. As regards at any rate the normal feeding habits of the two fish under notice, there is evidently much to be said for Colonel Bairnsfather's theory. He quaintly adds in further support of his view that mahseer might have to wait a long time for a dull day in India, while in some seasons trout in England would run serious risk of death from starvation if they were to refuse their food until the sun shone. The chief objection to this theory, in its practical application to deciding the chances of success, is the difficulty of determining what actually is the normal weather of some countries. If we take England, for instance, it is clear that the normal, or at any rate average, weather varies during cycles of years, for the English seasons have conspicuously changed even during the past quarter of a century. Our winters are nowadays far milder than they were in early - Victorian times, to judge at any rate from the rigours of Christmastide as depicted by Dickens and contemporary artists; and a succession of open weather on New Year's Eve has lent an old-fashioned and unnatural air to the orthodox pictures of snowbound coaches and frozen rivers.

Mr. Harvie-Brown on the deterioration of the British climate.

To men and women of normal tastes these are changes for the better, but there are other revolutions in the seasons, particularly in the springtide of the year, which fishermen cannot view with the same enthusiasm. Mr. J. A. Harvie-Brown, who has most kindly placed at my disposal two profusely annotated copies of *The Wonderful Trout*, attributes much of the falling-off in spring trout-fishing at the present day less to over-fishing than to the woeful deterioration of that once lovely season.

"Seeing," he writes, "that we have cold north winds now far into May, and that it is often only in small sheltered nooks and corners that any fly is seen to hatch off at all, the chances are again decreased. Often, when one angler confines his attention to some small sheltered reach and fishes it over and over again all day, killing a fair basket, another angler, only a few hundred yards away, neither gets a fish nor sees a single natural insect on the water."

The early part of 1905, particularly on the west side of Scotland, was too subject to spates to be in general favour with salmon-fishermen. One result was that salmon went right through short coast rivers, like the Awe, and found their way to higher waters, like (in this instance) those of the Orchy, without giving the rods below a chance of sport. The spring of 1905.

Nor is Mr. Harvie-Brown alone in his condemnation of the spring weather in recent seasons. Mr. Munro Edwards, writing with special reference to Lake Mr. Munro Edwards on the same subject.

Talyllyn, alludes to the same grievance as follows: "The hatch of light olive duns, which occurred formerly so regularly in May and June, is now exceedingly scarce, and naturally the trout take to cannibalism and bottom-feeding."

Weather lore n fishes.

Few aspects of the relations that exist in greater or less degree between fishing and the weather are more interesting, or, for the matter of that, of more practical importance, than the evidence for or against regarding certain game and coarse fish as weatherwise. The instinct which foretells coming changes of the weather is familiar in both wild and domestic animals, and few of those who live in the country are unfamiliar with such signs of rain as the sight of swallows flying near the ground or the sound of asses braying. It is not improbable that the significance of these alleged indications of bad weather is much overrated, but they are popularly accepted in this light, and many folks would sooner trust their infallibility than that of the barometer. At any rate, it is only what we should expect that animals living in a medium so sensitive to pressure as water should be in close sympathy with barometric variations. Many instances of their real or supposed power to forecast a change of weather for better or for worse will be found recorded in the following chapters. From Mold, in North Wales, two independent witnesses testify to the weatherwise talents of local trout. Colonel Davies-Cooke assures me that the fish have again and again foreseen and foretold a coming change from twelve to twenty-four hours before it was recorded by his Admiral Fitzroy barometer; and Major Wynn Eyton writes: "I have a small hatchery here, and on the morning of the 28th August last the small fishes would not come for their food. Even the big fishes, terrible gluttons, would hardly come to the surface for theirs. During the next twenty-four hours we had 1·28 inches of rain. It looks as if the fish were expecting a lot of bottom-food to come down and were waiting for it."

Colonel Davies-Cooke goes in greater detail into the behaviour of these and other fish in face of a coming change. Thus: "With a falling barometer, trout are sulky, in particular towards the close of a dry period. When the barometer is slowly dropping, both salmon and trout will leap high out of the water and are not feeding, only playing; and if by chance the angler gets a rise, it will be short." A falling barometer, indicating unsettled weather, is also fatal to grayling fishing. "Grayling," writes Mr. Rolt, whose monograph on this much-criticised fish is now in a second edition, "are influenced by atmospheric conditions more, probably, than any other freshwater fish. The morning may look promising enough, plenty of fly may hatch out, and every trout be on the move, but grayling, for some occult cause, cannot be induced to rise. On the return home, after a fruitless day, it may be

found that the barometer has steadily
fallen, and herein lies the explanation of
their perversity."

Many sea-fish, particularly those which, The late
like herrings and pilchards, move in shoals Matthias Dunn's
near the surface, and thus come in closer theory.
contact than most with the atmospheric
conditions, display sensibility to coming
storms. The late Matthias Dunn of
Mevagissey attributed this to the prompt-
ings of a special dermal sense, to which
he, in fact, added a seventh, the function
of which was to keep them informed of
the proximity of those magnetic headlands
which abut on the track of their migra-
tions. His views, though most ingenious
and based on a sincere conviction obvious
to all who knew him, did not find general
support in scientific circles, but the hypothesis of additional senses in some of
the inferior animals undoubtedly furnishes
a simple explanation for the marvellous
manifestations of what we vaguely describe
as their instinct.

Yet these same instincts are not in-

Norfolk trout
at fault :
Mr. Hall's
experience.
fallible. Mr. Hubert Hall has communicated a most interesting, because in some
ways unique, case of faulty weather-lore
in the trout of a Norfolk stream that he
has regularly fished for twelve years and
more. He thus states their case : " I
have been struck by the apparent inability
of fish to distinguish between a threatened
thunderstorm, which eventually bursts
upon the valley, and one which never
approaches within a distance of several
miles of the watershed. It is a well-
marked peculiarity of the purely local
climate that numberless summer storms,
or 'tempests,' as they are termed by the
natives, approach within a certain distance
of the valley and then pass out to sea.
The natives have long ceased to be
deceived by these indications, and even
cattle and birds show indifference to them,
except in the rare cases in which they are
destined to break in earnest upon the
thirsty soil. With the trout it is different.
They cease rising altogether and jump
frequently, with all the other symptoms

of electrical disturbance in the atmosphere. The eels are affected in a similar way, the obvious cause of uneasiness being the electricity in the air. Here at least is none of that prescience of a coming feast which is commonly attributed to their unfailing instinct." In view, however, of the fact that the conditions described in such interesting fashion by Mr. Hall are wholly exceptional, it is possible that he is unduly hard on the instinct of trout under more normal influences. It is, however, clear that Mr. Hall's intention is to raise a question of cause rather than effect, whether the sluggishness of fishes before an impending flood is due to the promise of food or to some physical shock to which they are peculiarly susceptible.

Of all the influences which make them- Sunshine. selves felt in the course of a day's fishing, none perhaps is more evident than the variations in the light and heat of the sun. The former affects the sight of the fish, and betrays to its suspicious eyes the shadow of the fisherman or the lurking dangers of his tackle. The latter is mainly important in bringing up a hatch of fly, but may also either stimulate or deaden the appetites of the fish. The generally accepted view of sunshine as an influence in trout fishing seems to be that intermittent gleams, with dark clouds in the intervals, are among the most favourable conditions. As regards salmon fishing, many anglers of experience, among them Sir Henry Seton-Karr, have no fault to find with a bright sun so long as it shines upstream, not down, from the back of the fish, that is to say, and not right in its eyes. The peculiar sunset glow, low on the water, is distinct from ordinary sunlight earlier in the day, and opinions differ as to its effect. Mr. Bagot dislikes it particularly for sea-trout, but with salmon Mr. Barker has had good results when the sun is setting, "and the light is warm and oblique." It goes perhaps without saying that any prejudicial effect which bright sunshine may have is diminished by discoloured, and heightened

by clear, water ; and consequently Mr.
Gathorne-Hardy regards sunshine as im-
material when the river is dirty.

There is in most fishes, in those more Is rising shor
particularly which are taken on the fly, a ^{due to light?}
tantalising trick, which we call "rising
short." On occasions the true explanation may no doubt lie in bad fishing, for
maladroitness on the part of the fisherman
may either frighten the fish or pull the fly
out of its reach. There are, however,
times when it is no fault of the angler
that as many as a score of fish in succession will rise at the fly without being
hooked. General Morton communicates
an interesting fact in connection with this
habit, to the effect that the sea-trout in
certain Scotch lochs regularly rise short
at a fixed time in the afternoon, usually
about 3 to 4 P.M., and a case of such
regularity points to some peculiar and
constant condition of the light striking
the surface of the water at a particular
angle. On one such occasion he counted
no fewer than twenty-one successive rises

without his landing a single fish. At first he attributed this to his own carelessness or want of skill, but he rejected this explanation on finding that he again hooked and landed his fish as soon as this period was over. It would no doubt be satisfactory if this annoying trick, which at times frustrates the fisherman's skill, baffles his resource, and sorely tries his patience, could be explained in the manner here suggested ; but it must at once be admitted that no such conclusion is warranted by the evidence at present available. It might, however, make a useful and interesting subject for independent inquiry.

Possible effect of solar eclipse.

None of those who have answered these questions make any reference, when dealing with the effect of sunshine, to the particular influence of a solar eclipse. The truth is that such a phenomenon occurs so rarely that fishermen have probably not had the opportunity of making any regular observations on its influence, if it has any, on fishing. As a personal experience of no particular value, I may just mention in passing that I was fishing for bass in the estuary of the Teign during most of the period of eclipse on August 30, 1905. In that river—we usually account a day of dead smooth water and glaring sun the best for catching the large bass—it was noticeable that, in spite of bright sunshine and the smoothest of water between 1 and 3 P.M., not a single bass was caught in the right way, though I ascertained that fish were in the river by accidentally foul-hooking one of about a pound weight. In that part of Devonshire at that hour very little of the eclipse was visible, save through smoked glass, and the sun shone oppressively. There was also a heavy, electrical feeling in the atmosphere, and it is probably this, whether connected with the eclipse or not, which put the fish down, as they never take the bait with thunder threatening.[1]

[1] Yet only a little farther down the coast, Mr. Minchin, fishing at the same time that day, found that whiting took the bait freely.—F. G. A.

Fish dazzled by sunshine.

The success which attends bass fishing, as has just been noted, on days of glaring sunlight has always seemed to me capable of explanation by the fact that they are dazzled by the sun. Bass, it must be borne in mind, enter estuaries like that of the Teign, not with any idea, like salmon, of ascending to the upper reaches to deposit their eggs, but solely in order to feed on the sand-eels and mackerel-fry, which they have previously followed into the brackish water. When, therefore, a hungry bass is dazzled by the glare of a July sun shining right in its eyes, it probably sees nothing but the bait, and for that it makes a dash without heeding the fine gut-line beyond. Sir Herbert Maxwell, whose researches into the question of vision in salmon and trout have prompted theories that have been widely discussed in angling circles, is also of opinion that fish, which have no eyelids to shield their eyes from the sun's glare, are peculiarly susceptible to this effect of dazzling.

Opinions are divided as to the precise manner in which a downpour of rain or hail may, directly or otherwise, affect the fisherman's chances.   It seems to be established that the majority of fish feed well during, at any rate, light showers, and some, like the mahseer, are said to feed on hailstones, occasionally even with fatal results.   As distinct from the imperfectly understood effect of a fall of rain or hail on the appetite of fish, we have in the course of the chapter on the subject to consider the indirect bearing of the rise of rivers in a spate, the discoloration of the water by floods, and the washing down of fresh stores of worms and other natural food.   Under certain conditions also the patter of rain-drops on the surface of dead still water may in some measure serve the fly-fisherman in place of a breeze, though whether, as generally believed, by hiding the cast, or, as Dr. Bright prefers to think, by more thoroughly oxidising the water, it is difficult to determine.

The question of the right level of each

particular river, or pool, which is what is
chiefly meant by the water being "in
order," is most interesting, and, unless
there is artificial damming, is, like the
colour of the water, directly dependent
on the rainfall. The condition of a river
settling down after a flood is a very
favourite one with experienced fishermen
in many localities, but evidence is given
in Chapter II. of some waters which yield,
if anything, even better sport under other
conditions and levels. Besides the condition which we call rain at normal temperatures and the extremely cold stage called
snow, which is more appropriately, together with frost, considered in the
following chapter, we shall in Chapter II.
take into account the effects of hail, while
Mr. Michelmore and others have something to say of the prejudicial effects of
certain clouds, which may be regarded as
rain in embryo.

Frost and
snow.
    Apart from the extreme condition of
ice, which, to any but a Samoyéde fishing
through ice-holes, precludes fishing alto-

gether, a very low temperature may not affect the appetite of the fish unfavourably. Grayling and chub appear to feed eagerly in frosty weather, and salmon are often caught freely on days that follow nights of frost.   Barbel, on the other hand, are rarely taken at all during wintry weather; and bream, though they may be creeled on mild days in the depth of winter, are also essentially summer and autumn fish. As regards snow, an actual fall seems less prejudicial to all manner of fishing than melting snow, or "snow-broth," in the water.   The evil effects of this melted snow cannot be a mere question of low temperature, since a sharp frost may do nothing to impede the capture of the very fish that sulk in pools tainted with the "broth."   Success in actual snowstorms, though chiefly noted in salmon fishing, is also recorded with sea-trout, Thames trout, brown trout, grayling, and roach. Even to the general rule of snow-broth being fatal to sport there are exceptions, for Mr. Rolt says that grayling will some-

Cases of good sport in "snow-broth."

times feed in spite of it, and Mr. Gallichan adds the interesting qualification that this is the case, in Derbyshire streams at any rate, only when the temperature falls below freezing-point, a condition under which grayling are apparently indifferent to this usually baneful influence. Brown trout are commonly regarded as more susceptible to the numbing effect of snow-water than even most other fish, but Mr. Gallichan mentions a case of a professional Welsh fisherman making a great catch of trout with the worm in spite of it, and Mr. Champneys once enjoyed many days of the best trout fishing that he ever had in a Scotch river during a succession of freshes caused by the melting of snow on warm nights. In connection with this experience he offers an interesting explanation, which will be found in Chapter III.

Wind. With reference to wind, we are concerned with its quantity and quality, and the latter, be it observed, is not always constant for any particular quarter; that is to say, the west wind may blow colder and harder on some waters than the east wind on others. For some fish, in both salt water and fresh, anglers prefer no wind at all. Lord Desborough, who had remarkable success with tarpon in Florida, found that his sport with that fish was best on still days. Mr. Sheringham likewise prefers a dead calm for roach, bream, tench, and perch. In most kinds of float-fishing excessive wind is for obvious reasons a drawback, just as in many forms of fishing with the artificial fly it is almost indispensable. For bass fishing in estuaries I prefer a dead calm, but in the open sea, particularly when fishing off rocky headlands, a curl on the water is productive of better results. The discomfort of too much wind in sea-fishing is too evident to need the support of evidence; but, generally speaking, the calmest days are best for pollack, bream, or whiting fishing at anchor, while in mackerel fishing from a boat under sail, as stiff a breeze as is compatible with easy management of the boat will generally be found to put the mackerel

on the feed, as well, no doubt, as to conceal the line in the broken wave-tops.
As regards the effect, favourable or the reverse, of winds from different quarters of the compass, much evidence will be found in Chapter IV., from which it will appear that not even the much-abused east wind is always as black as it is painted, since for Loch Leven, and some other waters similarly situated, it is not only not prejudicial to sport, but actually the best wind that can blow. It is a matter of opinion, with reference to this particular loch, whether the advantage of an east wind lies wholly in the fact that it suits the drifts on that east-and-west water, or whether it may not in part be due to its temperature being less harsh (since, on the east side of Scotland, it blows over the sea) than it is on western rivers. One correspondent describes it as a "much-libelled wind," and points out that whenever it blows upstream, it is likely to favour salmon and trout fishing more than a wind from any other quarter. In

the same way, since it is on that coast an offshore wind, and therefore ensures a calm sea, it is preferred to any other for sea-fishing on the west coast of Ireland, while at Brixham, on the other hand, it helps the bass-fisher in the opposite way, by giving the desirable curl to the water. The significance of the east wind, in fact, under a variety of accompanying conditions, is an excellent example of the absolute futility of any attempt to lay down hard and fast rules.

If anything can make an easterly wind still worse for fishing, where it is already bad, it is a touch of north in it. Though this, again, is not without many exceptions, a north-easterly wind probably has more enemies among fishermen than that blowing from any other quarter. Yet even in this detested wind success is not unknown, for Colonel M'Inroy once caught four salmon in such a wind in the course of an hour and a half, and, with the wind in the same quarter, Major Boulton remembers having, in the Outer

Hebrides, hooked no fewer than fourteen in a little over three hours' fishing. Touching trout, so high an authority on dry-fly fishing as Mr. Sydney Buxton has noticed "that the fish, perhaps invigorated and braced, will occasionally rise best with the N.E. wind, though casting is thereby rendered more difficult."

It is the winds from the south or west, or any point between the two, that have the warmest advocates among fishermen, who only favour the colder blasts under exceptional circumstances.

Thunder and lightning.

With thunder, as with rain, a distinction must be drawn between a storm actually in progress and another which threatens but may not burst in the immediate neighbourhood of the water fished. Mr. Hall's experience of Norfolk trout, unable to distinguish between the two conditions, has previously been noticed. As a general rule, and one with perhaps fewer exceptions than most of the rules formulated in these pages, it may be taken that most fish decline to feed when there is "thunder in the air," the peculiarly oppressive feeling in the atmosphere which precedes a storm apparently spoiling their appetites. This reluctance on their part to take a fly or bait immediately before the gathering of the storm does not, however, extend to the period when it is actually in progress, for Chapter V. will be found to contain frequent allusions to good sport during the most violent displays of lightning. Mr. Bagot on the North Tyne, Sir Ford North on the Irish Erne, Colonel Moore on the Slaney, General O'Callaghan on the Wansbeck (Northumberland), Mr. Gallichan in the Ardennes, Colonel Malcolm of Poltalloch on the Add, Mr. Coleridge on the Torridon, Mr. Dodd in the Black Forest, Mr. Noble on the Blackadder, and others, chronicle good catches of salmon or trout during storms of greater or less severity, and Mr. Wheeley caught one of his best Thames trout under similar conditions. The common eel is not a fish calculated to attract many sportsmen to the waterside, but those who find their pleasure in its capture will note that more than one correspondent draws attention to the fact that thunder is good for eels.

Fog and mist. The personal discomfort (which in country like the Devonshire moorland becomes actual danger) of going fishing in a fog is so obvious as to need no comment. What concerns us more closely in the present volume is the direct influence of fogs and mists on fishing. Mist on the hills is, according to the evidence given in Chapter VI., generally fatal to sport, whether in the salmon-pools of the Aberdeenshire Dee or Argyllshire Awe, on the Torridon, on the Itchen, or on the lakes of Norway. Yet, during a foggy October morning on the Spey, Sir Ford North caught two salmon in three-quarters of an hour, and, coming to coarse-fishing, Mr. R. B. Marston recalls having on one occasion caught roach as fast as he could land them, though the fog was so dense at the time that he could hardly see his float. Mr. Basil Champneys regards mist on the water as fatal in dry-fly fishing, though not necessarily prejudicial to the wet fly, a distinction for which he gives a very reasonable explanation.

As regards sea-fishing, I doubt whether fog has much effect on, at any rate, ground-fish, though, as it is not usual to leave the shore with any menace of fog in evidence, opportunities of judging its influence are very few. More than once, however, I have been surprised when at anchor by a passing fog, during which the safest course is just to remain on the ground till the land clears; and on one occasion at any rate the tedium of waiting was relieved by some of the fastest whiting fishing that I ever remember having. I do not, however, attribute this to the effect of the fog, but merely to my having anchored on a particularly good ground near the Eddystone and to the whiting being that afternoon on the feed.

From the foregoing summary of the lines on which the present inquiry has been prosecuted, it would seem as if most

What, then, is bad fishing weather?

fish can at one time or another be caught in practically any weather. "Not one of the conditions that you name," writes Mr. Gathorne-Hardy, "would keep me from the riverside if the water were in order." It may therefore occur to the reader to ask : What day, then, is really bad for fishing ? "Apart from the intermittent appetite of a trout," writes Sir Henry Seton-Karr, as if in answer to the question, "the usually accepted adverse conditions are a bright sun, and, if on a lake, smooth water, also east wind or thunderstorms." Yet, as will be shown, not one of these real or supposed drawbacks is without its exceptions. Frankly, the fisherman's bad day is just the day on which he cannot catch any fish, neither more nor less. It has, we shall perceive, nothing whatever to do with the bad days of other folks. Indeed, what other people call bad weather may seem ideal to the fisherman. Colonel Deane and others, who like a perfect gale for lake-fishing, would hardly find the ordinary tourist of their opinion, and the average preference for an overcast day to one of uninterrupted sunshine argues eccentricity to the lay mind. The angler may therefore revel in what other folk regard as hideous weather. "The best sort of day for this loch," said a keeper in reply to Colonel Malcolm's inquiry, "the best sort of day, Kornel, is a real *beast* of a day"! That, then, which is miserable weather to the ordinary understanding may give the fisherman the chance of his lifetime. Indeed, this indifference to dirty weather may even assume a more acute phase, in which, it is to be feared, the fisherman figures in a very selfish light. Rain and storms, as Mr. Wheeley points out, while having no terrors for the angling enthusiast, keep other folks at home, and in much-frequented waters, like those of the Lower Thames, this may mean immunity from the madding crowd of motor-boats and other pleasure-craft, a privilege which fishermen may think cheaply bought at the price of a wetting.

Other conditions besides those enumerated.

Doubtless there are other conditions of the water and atmosphere beyond those enumerated in the queries addressed to those who have made such generous response. As a case in point, there is the possible influence of distant earthquakes, as suggested by Mr. Sheringham. Sir John Edwards-Moss also refers to "an atmospheric peculiarity, which you do not mention, that peculiar blue haze, like London milk, which one sometimes gets with a S.E. wind"; and he gives an instance in which, though usually regarding this as a hopeless condition for fishing, he once tried his luck in it, and killed no fewer than six salmon on a Silver Doctor on his beat on the Naver. Yet another strange and hitherto unexplained phenomenon, familiar to the majority of fishermen, is referred to by Colonel Davies-Cooke in the following terms :—

"I have one more subject to touch on, not mentioned in your letter, and that is those most peculiar movements, nearly

always in squally weather, as of some fish
darting swiftly right across, and just
beneath, the surface. I have watched
them for years and have never seen a fish,
or found any one who has traced them
to fish, so I conclude that the movements
are not, in fact, to be so explained. I
should like to see the subject discussed.
All that I am certain about is, that when
these eccentricities are about, the basket
will not be full."

Most of those who have contributed to
this volume devote their remarks to the
salmon and trout, while a few say something of pike and coarse fish. To sea-
fishing the references are few. Had the
effects of weather on the fisherman,
rather than on the fish, been under discussion, sea-fishing must, for obvious and
disagreeable reasons, have assumed a far
more important place. As it is, however,
even the marine fishes sought by the
amateur dwell in most cases at depths
commonly regarded as lying beyond the
influence of atmospheric changes. This,

Weather and
sea-fishing.

however, is far from being the case. Two correspondents thus state their somewhat divergent views on the subject :—

Writing of sea-fishing off the Isle of Man, Professor Boyd Dawkins considers that "the question of light is the most important. This is largely due to the fact that fish can see the line if there be plenty of light. The temperature of the water is another important factor in the question of fish biting or not. I do not think that the wind affects their mood, except by ruffling the surface and thus confusing the light below. I doubt whether the fog exerts any influence, except by obscuring the light. The fish, in my opinion, feed after intervals of rest and at different states of the tide at different places. . . . As a rule, the fish feed best on the first two hours of the flood in the seas round the Isle of Man."

On the other hand, the Rev. W. A. Mathews writes with reference to his experiences of bays on the bold York-shire coast :—

"Sea-fish seem to feel the same influences of the winds as their brothers in the shallower waters of streams, and will bite freely when a W. or S.W. wind is blowing, though they will touch nothing when the breezes are from N. or E., even at depths where it might be thought that the wind could not make itself felt."

John Bickerdyke thus sums up his views on the question :— John Bickerdyke's views.

"So far as salmon fishing is concerned, the best weather is that which gives the best light and the best water. That is to say, we first of all want rain to rise the water and make the fish run ; then a less quantity of rain to keep the river steady and up to a certain level, when the fish usually take. Salmon take badly when the river is rising rapidly or falling rapidly. The light, too, is most important, the fish apparently not seeing the fly, or not caring to see it when the clouds are very low and the sky is much overcast. A bright sky, on the other hand, is bad, because probably the fish see the gut and that the fly is an artificial production, and not something good to eat or worthy of attack. It follows that ideal salmon fishing conditions are none too common.

"When fly - fishing for trout, undoubtedly the best weather is that which produces the largest number of natural flies on the water. Sea-trout feed all the more readily if there is rain causing a slight freshet, or when the water is clearing a little after a big one. Trout dislike bright sunlight combined with clear calm water, and at such times usually retire to shady places. But I have caught them many times when the sun has been bright by fishing fine and upstream.

"For grayling fishing, nothing beats a slightly frosty night followed by a calm, mild, hazy day.

"In pike fishing there seems no particular rule as to the weather, but the fish are most voracious after a spell of thick water, during which they presumably have not been able to get much food, for they hunt by sight and are then in the position of a greyhound having to catch a hare in a thick fog. On lakes and still reaches, wind decidedly helps the angler. For coarse fish generally, the weather which gives abundance of water in a river without it being too thick is usually good, provided that fishing is bad, as a rule, during storms. Nothing seems to bring the fish more steadily on the feed than a long spell of settled weather if the water is not too low. Roach, however, always bite best after rain, as do perch. In summer, chub and gudgeon take best in fine sunny weather. Modern perch, though generally hungry, are shy and cautious to a degree. Like pike, they take best after a thick flood and probably for the same reason.

"Sea-fish do not seem to me to be influenced by weather as much as by the state of the tide, and by the abundance or scarcity of food on their feeding-ground. Storms seem to drive them away from the coast; but bass are to be caught inshore in the open sea in thick water after such disturbances."

The moral of this book.

If the testimony collected in the following chapters may be condensed into one piece of advice it is, that the angler should never be discouraged from trying his luck by any weather condition condemned by the text-books, but should persist in the face of apparently hopeless circumstances. A too careful attention to the face of the sky may at times baulk the over-cautious fisherman of what might, by trusting a little more to luck, have been a red-letter day. In support of this advice the following pages contain many anecdotes, yet none perhaps more striking than the following, for which I am indebted to Mr. Russell. As it concerns so eminent a fisherman as the late Francis Francis, it may possibly have appeared in print elsewhere; if so, I reproduce it here with apologies. Mr. Francis was fishing Loch Lomond with Mr. Brown, late Secretary of the Loch

Lomond Angling Association, and one day, when the sky was flecked with white clouds, and a cold, hard wind blew on the surface of the loch, they agreed that fishing under such conditions would be folly, and therefore stayed away from the water.   Other anglers, with less experience to warn them, went forth, in spite of conditions obviously unfavourable to expert eyes, and though no trout (the chief fish of the loch, and the one, no doubt, to which Mr. Francis's doubts referred) were caught, it proved to be one of the best salmon days of the season.   This little story illustrates at once the importance of the fisherman trying his luck in all weathers and the indifference of salmon to conditions of wind and weather that adversely affect trout.   The fact is, the angler never knows his luck on even the most unpromising of days. The Bishop Suffragan of Swansea, who has fished these thirty years in the Towy and other Welsh rivers, tells me that his best salmon, a 24 lb. fish, was hooked "on a very bright sunny morning, when it was almost hopeless to expect anything. But my fly was carried by the stream quite under a bush, and there the fish was hooked."

" It must," writes Sir Henry Seton-Karr, " have happened to all salmon-fishermen occasionally to flog good water, well stocked with fish, in good order, and under apparently perfect weather conditions, to no purpose whatever. On the other hand, I have killed chance salmon on the Erne in July, in clear, smooth water, under a blazing sun, which shone, however, upstream and not down ; that is to say, from behind the fish, and not in their eyes. Also, I have killed them in a snowstorm, on the Eden, in April. I am almost inclined to the bold assertion that, if the salmon are there, and not too intent on running, but settled for the time in a pool, there is always some hope of a rise, whatever weather conditions prevail—that is, of course, provided the fly is cannily chosen of a size to suit the depth and colour of the water, and artistically thrown over the fish."

It is therefore of great importance that the fisherman who would be successful should persist in the teeth of the elements; that he should go forth undismayed and stay by the water as long as he can see to fish.

"A successful fisherman," writes Dr. Foakes-Jackson, "must not be given to too much observation of the conditions of the weather. It is as true of fishing as it is of agriculture : ' He that observeth the wind shall not sow, and he that regardeth the clouds shall not reap.' Not to go out fishing because the day is not a likely one is a fatal mistake. There are, of course, certain climatic conditions under which it is impossible to catch fish; but the weather, as a rule, changes so frequently and so rapidly that it is generally worth waiting for these to alter. Often under apparently perfect conditions no fish stirs, and the only thing to be done is to fish on till a chance comes. There is a loch in

Ross-shire on which the fish are said never to rise well. Nevertheless, if a man knows the water and is prepared to work hard all day, he can generally fill his basket. This is true of most lochs."

With regard to the reluctance of trout to rise "under apparently perfect conditions," I recollect one August day on Loch Etive, when I fished for hours in company with Mr. Mayo Robson, who, along with the Craig shooting, held fishing rights in the Noe and Liver, both of which fall into that beautiful loch. The prevailing weather, a strong westerly wind and unceasing fine rain, was locally regarded as perfect, yet the fish were obdurate, and only a few very small individuals rose, spasmodically and mostly short. Yet on the day before, with bright sunshine and not a ripple on the surface—anything, in short, but promising conditions—I had found small sea-trout rising freely.

The whole moral of this book, then, is to persist. As one correspondent says:

"Provided the river is not in flood, and given the presence of fish in season and stream enough to carry the fly, no weather conditions should altogether damp the ardour or destroy the hope of the salmon-fisherman."

The undoubted weather-lore of trout, at any rate in some localities, is an additional argument in favour of remaining by the waterside, since, even if the conditions be unfavourable at the moment, the sensitive fish may be aware of a coming change for the better, unsuspected by the fisherman, and feed accordingly just when he would by all his rules expect them most to sulk. As Major Wynn Eyton says: "Trout may have certain times and conditions for feeding, but a sudden change in the weather may upset the rule." Any sort of change, in fact, may bring luck to the salmon-angler. Mr. Conner relates how, on a dull, cloudy day in July, on the Bandon River—an abrupt change after a bright, dry spell, with no fish taking—five fish were killed, though there was no rise in the water.

"The man," so another correspondent puts it, "with plenty of time and patience will often catch fish at unexpected times, whereas he who only goes to the river at the most favourable times, and rushes away if the fish are not feeding, often misses the rise altogether. The latter may be a better fisherman, but the more patient man will get the fish in the end."

It is quite useless to sit idle on the chance of better things to come. It is better, indeed, to stay away from the river altogether than to wait on fortune on the banks without putting your tackle together. Those beginners who have been taught to regard certain kinds of wind and weather as hopeless for fishing may, if they have the patience to turn the following pages, take heart from the cases of success, sometimes even of record bags, under precisely these forbidding conditions, and may be encouraged to try conclusions with the hope of results as satisfactory. The essence of success is perseverance in defiance of such real or imaginary drawbacks. "Ye'll no catch fush," quoth Mr. Coleridge's gillie, putting the case in a nutshell, "wi' your fly on the bank"!

CHAPTER I

SUNSHINE

I. Light. — Effect on the colour of the water—On the
sight of fishes—How far can a fish see?—Fish dazzled
by sunlight—Use of torches in sea-fishing—Evidence
in favour of sunshine—A good day on Loch Assynt—
Two deadly methods of trout fishing — Conflicting
opinions—Sunshine an advantage in cold weather and
spring fishing—Its influence varies according to season
—A blazing day on the Tweed—Two successes in sunshine on the Torridon; another on the Bann River
—Rainbow-trout in Minnesota—Advantage of sun and
cloud alternately—Rivers on which sunshine is fatal
—Lochs of the Outer Hebrides—Other small lakes
—Curious mistrust of gut—Special considerations of
sunset.

II. Heat.—Direct and indirect influence of heat—Excessive drought a bar to fishing—Case of India—Trout
in lakes—Loch Lomond—Various opinions—Difficulty
of generalising — Hot weather favourable in the
eastern counties; in Norway; for pike in a reservoir;
for char in Loch Tay — Mahseer may sulk in hot
weather—Other fish lethargic—Importance of temperature of water being higher than temperature
of air.

In most human beings there is implanted
some survival of pagan sun-worship, nor

are the latest discoveries of the therapeutic
magic worked by the sun's rays likely to
lessen our faith in that source of all
natural light and heat. Those of us who
have in the Great Desert cowered from
his fierceness under burnouse or tent may
also have feared it, but the instinctive
reverence for the sun is not altered. Yet,
agreeable though its warmth and brightness makes indulgence in any outdoor
pursuit, the sun is not invariably a friend
to the fisherman, who always fears its
light, as betraying his guile, and sometimes also has reason to resent its heat, as
spoiling either the condition of the water
or the appetites of the fish.

I. LIGHT

Although, as will presently be shown,
a number of experienced anglers attach
great importance to the effect of temperature, chiefly, of course, as affecting the
hatch of fly on the water, it is generally
agreed that light is an all - important
influence in many kinds of angling.

In considering the part played by light, it is necessary to take into account the colour of the water and the range of vision in fishes.

Most fishermen, and those particularly who have sought their sport on lakes, must at times have noticed strange and even inexplicable tints in the water, which may be perfectly clear and not discoloured with peat or any other familiar substance. That these hues, blue or black, are directly responsible for bad sport is improbable. They must be regarded rather, as Mr. Earl Hodgson would say, as symptomatic of some condition, or set of conditions, un-determined, but realised as prejudicial. General Dalton recalls that in all his salmon fishing in both Canada and Nor-way he never liked "a black look in the water, which sometimes results from special atmospheric conditions. Often when thunder is imminent, or in stormy and unsettled weather, one gets the water in an unsatisfactory black state."

This blackness is not a question of

depth, like the darker blue of deep sea water, or the dark colour of Highland lochs, which Stewart considered of assistance in concealing the fisherman's tackle. It seems to depend rather on reflections.

"For lake-fishing," writes Mr. Beale Adams, who, as an artist, naturally studies this aspect of the ruling conditions, "colour seems an important point to me. I do not mean peat stain, or anything of that sort, but sky reflections. My fishing days are simply determined by whether I think the water a good colour." Another artist sends me an opinion on a somewhat different effect of light on the details of fishing. Mr. Dendy Sadler, who has a special corner in the fisherman's sanctum, is a firm believer in the old maxim, "A dull day, a bright fly; a bright day, a dull fly," which is, however, on some well-known waters, advisedly reversed in practice.

That these colours of the water are not themselves hostile to fish taking the fly, but are rather a case of Mr. Earl Hodgson's symptoms, is sufficiently clear at any rate in the case of the Torridon, which, Mr. Coleridge says, is usually hopeless for fishing when the water is blue and clear *from melting snow.* The italics are mine, but the evidence clearly shows that lack of sport has nothing to do with blue water, but depends solely on the hostile influence of snow-broth (see Chapter III.), of which that hue is but the outward symbol.

On the sight of fishes.

When we come to a consideration of how far fishes can see, and how, precisely, they view a fly or other object alighting on the surface, we have to speculate with very meagre data. We do not even know for certain whether a salmon lying at the bottom of a pool can see an angler standing on the bank unless his shadow falls on the water. We surmise, indeed,

How far can a fish see?

from internal evidence that it can. Yet it has been contended, even, I believe, demonstrated, by a German anatomist that a salmon cannot see farther under water than six inches, measured horizontally. What the fisherman, however, has to consider for practical purposes is the range at which a fish can see an object interposed overhead between it and the sun or sky. Even if six inches be the very modest horizon of the salmon under water, it will rise at a fly from the bottom of a pool many times that depth. The effect of an insufficiently or excessively illuminated background may be such as to magnify or reduce its size, distort its shape, and obscure its colouring, the last to such an extent as to render the fish to all intents and purposes colour-blind. Extremes of light may be equally unfavourable to salmon fishing; for, with an overcast sky and low clouds, the fish either do not, or will not, see the fly, and, on the other hand, given a bright sky, they may see too much.

The view commonly held as to the effect of bright light is that it frustrates the angler's purpose by betraying himself and his tackle to the fish—an opinion that, no doubt, receives support from the success which often under such conditions

Fish dazzled by sunlight.

attends the use of small flies and fine tackle. There is, however, an alternative possibility which we must reckon with, and this is the dazzling of the fish by the sun shining full in its eyes. These, as Sir Herbert Maxwell reminds me, are unprotected by lids, and are therefore peculiarly susceptible to the glare. Dazzling may operate in one of two ways. It may prevent the fish from seeing even the lure, and with salmon which are not actually feeding, but merely rising in half-hearted and wanton fashion at the fly, this is in all likelihood its effect. On the other hand, with fish like the bass, of which I have caught all my best in gin-clear water and glaring July weather, it may just dazzle the fish to the extent of hiding the tackle and hook. The bass has no ambition to ascend to the higher reaches of the river so long as it finds abundance of sand-eels and other fry in the estuary, and it is not therefore so easily baulked of its meal as the salmon.

As was, however, said above, our knowledge of the sight of fishes and of the precise effect which natural or artificial light may exercise upon their eyes is for the most part guesswork. In some seas, for example, in which I have fished, torch-light is largely employed by night, with the object of keeping the shoal of mackerel or other fish round the boats. This implicit faith in the attractiveness of a flare hung over the bow is shared by Spanish, Portuguese, and Italians, all of whom are efficient fishermen, and I have felt the benefit of the practice in different parts of the Mediterranean, as well as on the coast of Madeira.

Mr. Brown has, however, come to a different conclusion with regard to artificial illumination as an aid to fishing in the sea. " I have," he writes, " when pulling about in shallow water, put a torch over the bow of the boat, and seen fish quietly swimming about below, not minding the boat or flare. After fishing for sea-bream one evening in fourteen fathoms, getting moderate sport, the fish ceased taking at dark, and I put down an electric lamp to try if it would light them to their supper or otherwise attract them. None took a bite at all, and I concluded that in this case perhaps the light scared them away, as its glow might suggest the phosphorescence caused by the movements of some large fish, potentially an enemy." Mr. Brown's inference of his submarine lamp suggesting the proximity of a shark or hake is ingenious, but the case of a torch suspended over the water cannot be regarded as analogous, as light from such a source must certainly have a different effect from that of a lamp under water. At any rate, I satisfied myself of the beneficial effect of the flare on mackerel and scad, off Funchal, on more than one April night, by trying, always without success, to catch even a single fish on the dark side of the boat. I was further convinced that these fish fed much nearer the surface in the artificial torchlight than they had done before sundown in the natural light of day. To catch

them at all by daylight, it is necessary to plunge nearly the whole bamboo
rod vertically under water—a curious
position according to our ideas, but one
with which a very little practice ensures
familiarity. At first, indeed, I resented
this injunction, with the result that I
caught nothing, while natives in the same
boat jerked a fish on board every few
seconds. As soon as the torches are all
alight, the joint illumination of fifty or
sixty boats anchored every evening on
the same ground brings the fish so close
to the surface that the rods may be used
in the ordinary way.

Although bright sunshine is, on the
whole, regarded in no friendly way by
fishermen, some of the evidence of my
correspondents indicates that it is, con-
ditionally or otherwise, an advantage
with salmon, and sometimes also with
trout. Its influence even varies according to place and season, and whereas it
is found to favour sport in the eastern
counties and in spring salmon-fishing,

elsewhere and at other times of the year it is less welcome. Even those, however, who would rather under normal conditions have a dull day, admit exceptional cases of good sport in dazzling sunlight.

Evidence in favour of sunshine. Sir George Brown boldly asserts that all his best days with trout have been in sunshine and east wind. This is perhaps the most unqualified praise bestowed, although Mr. Sheringham prefers sunny days for perch and grayling, and it also suits General Dalton best with clear water for fishing with worm or shrimp, though necessarily with very fine tackle.

A good day on Loch Assynt. "The best trouting day," writes Prof. Burkitt, "that we had during the season of 1905 was a bright day with a fair wind, 23rd Aug. We were on the Skaig beat of Loch Assynt, and the water was so clear and blue that it was hard to believe that a fish could fail to see the cast as well as the fly. But we caught some dozen while this bright time lasted (about 1 to 3.30), the largest a two-pounder.

Several other good baskets of trout were made that day."

Sir Henry Pottinger refers to two Two deadly methods of trout fishing. deadly modes of catching trout in hot weather, not very far removed from poaching, and indeed interdicted on some waters reserved for the fly, yet very tempting when not a fish can be moved by more sporting means. Both of these may be said to depend on sunshine in great measure for their success. The first of them is upstream worm-fishing, which is most successful on the hottest and brightest days, with the water very low and clear. "In this style, which is in vogue among professional fishermen in the north of England, the fisherman wades cautiously up the bed of the stream, and, with a rather stiff rod, flicks his bait a short distance in front of him, letting it run down with the current." The other style, likewise helped by heat and sunshine, is known as "shade-fishing," in which, during the hottest days, "the angler creeps along the bank of the

river, concealing himself behind bushes
and tree-trunks, and drops into the deep
holes a minnow artistically impaled on a
hook with a leaded shank. The bait is
then repeatedly drawn nearly to the
surface and allowed to dive again. By
it the old trout, which are lurking in the
deep water under the bank, are attracted
to their doom and must, when they have
taken the minnow, be allowed to gorge it
quietly for some minutes"!

Conflicting
opinions.

Even those who, under given conditions, either prefer or tolerate sunshine,
differ in many matters of detail, as the
two following remarks illustrate :—

" I do not mind sunshine when fishing
a lake for trout, *provided the sun is not
directly facing me* and there is a good
breeze to ruffle the water." (C. E. M. E.)

" In bright sunshine, *provided the angler
has the sun in his face*, so that the shadow
of his rod and line do not fall on the
water, sport is frequently excellent."
(H. A. R.)

The italics are my own.

Most of those who favour bright sunshine for their fishing qualify their preference with some sort of conditions. On the Kent (Westmorland) and North Tyne (Northumberland), for instance, Mr. Bagot says that the afternoon sun alone puts down salmon and sea-trout, even after a good rise, the morning sun being less prejudicial to sport. Mr. Gathorne-Hardy has no objection to bright sunshine if the water is dirty. Mr. Conner, writing of the Bandon River, prefers it indeed in conjunction with a high wind, but without any wind at all experience has shown him that it is usually fatal. It seems, moreover, that sunshine may be better for the fisherman in a low than in a high temperature. This at any rate is the opinion of Sir John Edwards-Moss, who thinks it an advantage in cold weather, when the water is on the big side, though generally hopeless in warm weather and low water. In very early spring, when the fish are perhaps less critical of tackle than they are later in

Sunshine an advantage in cold weather and spring fishing.

the year, he also regards sunshine as "almost a good condition." In frost, also, he thinks that it may improve the angler's chances.

Salmon also rise well at times in bright sun in the Sand River, and Mr. Dodd not merely prefers bright sun to white clouds, but has found it no bar to good sport when dry-fly fishing for both trout and grayling.

Its influence varies according to season. That the influence of sunshine varies, as above suggested, with the time of year is only perhaps what we should expect. Dr. Charles Chree writes that, "in the streams of West Forfarshire and East Perthshire, trout take the worm very readily in bright sunshine in the month of June, so long as the angler uses fine gut and fishes from his knees, so as to keep out of sight." A month later, he adds, it would under normal conditions be exceedingly difficult to make a decent catch. General O'Callaghan also says something of these seasonal differences in the part played by sunshine. "In the

Mayfly time," he writes, "the absence of either cloud or sun seems to make little difference. Given sufficient warmth to hatch out the fly, fish rise just as freely on a sunny as on a cloudy day. I have made a good basket in June on an absolutely cloudless day. At other times, cloud *with warmth* is an advantage, since it makes the gut of the casting line less conspicuous; and towards the end of the hot weather the evening is the only time of day when one can hope to rise fish. In the early part of the season, sun is a necessity, since without it no fly is hatched. At that time, as well as in September, I have always found that fish rise best between 11 A.M. and 3 P.M. As with a dry-fly, I believe sun to be an advantage in wet-fly fishing, both at the beginning and at the end of the season. In the hotter summer months, cloud is a necessity, though, with a light upstream wind, fine tackle, and one small fly, I have made good baskets on many days, even late in June."

Many of those who recognise that bright sun is more often than not a handicap are able to quote exceptions from their own experiences.

A blazing day on the Tweed.

Sir Herbert Maxwell, for instance, can recall a day on the Tweed (29th Oct. 1891), with blazing sun, low water, and hard frost. So brilliant was the light that he could see fish lying in the Craig-over Pool at Mertoun, and of his own uninfluenced judgment he would in all probability have left them where they lay, thinking any endeavour to move them hopeless. But his boatman persuaded him to put a small fly over them on a very long line, with the result that he hooked three fish and landed two, respectively 18 lbs. and 16 lbs. He also remembers the unexpected happening with trout, and an odd big fish coming to the creel in a blazing noon of summer sunshine on a loch—a state of things in which he would ordinarily counsel putting off fishing operations until nightfall.

Mr. Coleridge contributes an interest-

ing experience of two occasions, both of Two suc-
which he regards as exceptional, on which cesses in sun-
shine on the
he took salmon from the Torridon (Ross- Torridon ;
shire) in blazing sunlight, and the accompanying conditions displayed, as will
be seen, some other differences, which
must be taken into account.

"The first was in a still, deep pool,
no ripple, water moderately thick, and
just after a cloud had passed away from
the sun at my back. I was fishing from
a low bank, where there are no trees, and
standing three or four yards back from
the edge. The other time was in a still,
shallow pool, so clear that I had just been
trying to see the fish lying on the bottom.
I put a fly into the ripple, just where the
stream flowed in at the head of the pool,
and a fish of about 12 lbs. came out four
times from my side of the bank. After
due rests, I hooked him at the fifth cast.
The sun was facing me, and though I
was hidden by the high bank, it seemed
as if the rod-top, line, cast, and hook
must be visible to the fish."

In the first of these cases, it will be noticed that the sun was behind the fisherman and that the water was both deep and dirty. On the second occasion, he had the sun in front, and the water was shallow and clear. These details are of importance in the light of what has gone before.

another on the Bann River.

Sir Thomas Esmonde recollects on one occasion killing six or seven dozen brown trout on the Bann River, near Gorey, one day in March, in bright sunshine and a north wind. There are, in fact, numerous instances of success in sunshine. The late Canon Beechey wrote to me not long before his death that, while he considered a bright day, with blue sky and roving wool-pack clouds, the very worst for fly-fishing, he had known other anglers, fishing in some favoured spot, do well under such conditions. Sir James Fergusson has more than once, to his own surprise, with fine tackle and small flies, caught salmon on sunny days, with little breeze, and Mr. Sheild has also taken them with a March Brown and other trout-flies, even in low, bright water and hot sun, with fish jumping in the pools— the kind of day that he ordinarily regards as hopeless.

As regards trout, which are stay-at- Rainbow-home animals, a good deal depends on trout in Minnesota. the extent of their education in the ways of the fisherman. Sir Henry Seton-Karr once made a fine basket of rainbow-trout in a private fishery, not far from Minne-apolis, in calm, clear water on a sunny August day. He would not have thought such a result possible, and fished only to oblige his American friends, who were sanguine of success.

Whatever objections fishermen may Advantage o have learnt from experience to raise sun and clou alternately. against sunshine, there seems to be no doubt whatever about a condition of alter-nating sun and shade, with gleams between passing clouds, being particularly favour-able to sport, and preferable even to uniform dulness of the sky. What pre-cisely may be the effect of such chopping and changing of the light on the vision of fishes we cannot know, but the results, as measured by the catch, are almost invariably satisfactory. The following are some extracts from letters touching on the point :—

"Late in March, or early in April, I have supposed gleams of sunshine to have encouraged fish to take the fly, but this may have only meant that it rendered the artificial fly more visible, or else that it may have brought out the natural fly in sufficient numbers to make it worth while for the trout to turn their attention in that direction." (C. C.)

"Sunshine, *broken*, is good on the Bucks Chess and Coln." (J. J. D.)

"Bright intervals of sunshine are good for loch-trout in Orkney. If *generally* bright, a passing cloud will often make the fish take. If *generally* dull, a glint of sun has the same effect." (A. M. S. G.)

"Trout-fishing in the Loch of Girlsta (Shetland) is better for occasional bright glimpses of sunshine, as well as in Ting-

A SMALL BUT GOOD POOL

wall. With other Shetland lochs, where the land around is high, sunshine at the angler's back is always fatal." (J. S. T.)

"For fly-fishing, sunshine should be pale and fitful." (W. M. G.)

"For practically all fish other than grayling, carp, bream, tench, and perch, I like April weather, sun chasing clouds, clouds compelling sun." (H. T. S.)

On some waters, however, it seems that sunshine is generally, if not invariably, fatal to sport, particularly if combined with some other condition of wind or cloud. The following are cases:—

For spring salmon in Scotland generally when combined with east wind (C. E. D.), for salmon-fishing in the Tay (W. O. D.), and, with white fleecy clouds, for the Aberdeenshire Dee (R. T. C.). Between 10 A.M. and 2 P.M. it is considered, except in rough and broken water, fatal to sport in the streams and smaller rivers of Banff-shire (J. C.), and scarcely more hopeful, even with a good breeze, for lake-fishing

Rivers on which sun-shine is fatal

in Donegal (W. E.-J.). Except in short, strong runs, it also renders fishing hopeless in the Upper Tawe, Carmarthenshire (W. W. F.), and as a rule it also puts a stop to trout fishing on Loch Leven (W. R.).

Lochs of the Outer Hebrides. "In the lochs of the Outer Hebrides," writes Major Boulton, "it is seldom any good fishing for salmon in bright sunlight. Out of over 200 caught in three seasons in a loch in the Lewes, I do not think that more than a dozen were caught when the sun was out, and these were all small fish." Of sea-trout, on the other hand, he and a friend took upwards of 500 in one season in the Lewes, and under all conditions, but the best baskets were always made on dull days.

Other small lakes. That bright sunshine is more fatal in small, still lakes than in running water is only what we should expect. Sir Douglas Brooke tells me that he has a small lake on his grouse mountain so crammed with very small trout that he has before now, "without fishing very energetically," killed twelve dozen of them in a day. Yet, even with such greedy hordes in the water, bright sunshine effectually puts an end to sport, and not a trout can be caught in it. Mr. Black writes that it is likewise hopeless to fish during sunny weather in a small artificial loch, well stocked with Loch Levens, a few miles from Edinburgh.

If these coincidences of sunshine and bad sport are to be attributed wholly to the fierce light thrown on the fisherman's gut, it is very singular, when one comes to think of it, that the fish, which take no notice of leaves, straws, even branches and coarser flotsam, should be so suspicious of even thick gut. It might be thought that even the reel-line would pass muster side by side with such natural objects, but for fine gut to inspire fear is simply marvellous, and suggests a degree of discrimination which is hardly in harmony with the organisation and sensibilities of that class. Yet the fact that when a breeze ruffles the surface of the

Curious mistrust of gut.

water a glaring sun is often no bar to sport, seems to demonstrate that this betrayal of the gut and hook is the only explanation of a trout's aloofness in bright light and still water, and that another correspondent's view, that the service rendered by the breeze is merely to stimulate the appetite of the fish, by oxygenation, is untenable.

Before leaving the influence of sunlight, something must be said of the special condition of sunset, when the oblique and failing rays appear to produce a different effect from that of the earlier hours of the day. The following opinions on sunset and kindred conditions of light are of interest in this connection and illustrate divergent views :—

Special con-
siderations of
sunset.

"I have never succeeded much in bright sunshine with either salmon or sewin;[1] but when the sun goes down, after a bright day in July or August, fish will take well." (C. E. M. E.)

[1] *I.e.* sea-trout, the "peal" of Devonshire rivers (F. G. A.).

"The sunset glow on the water, I find, is very bad in sea-trout fishing. The moon, on the contrary, would seem favourable to night-fishing for sea-trout,[1] at any rate on the Kent (Westmorland), where I have done most of my night-fishing." (R. B.)

"I had fished a stream in the south of Ireland, which was full of small trout, all day without success. It was a bright day, not good for fly-fishing, and I could only stir a few very small fish. Suddenly, about an hour before sunset, the water seemed to boil with fish. At each cast I hooked one, or even two, as the flies were seized the moment they touched the water. This went on till my basket was filled. The fish were exactly the same weight, half a pound. The light was just beginning to fade when this began, and it was dark when I left off." (A. D. C.)

"I have known salmon rise particularly well when the sun is about setting and the light is warm and oblique. It is little

[1] Not for conger (F. G. A.).

use fishing in the Namsen River (Norway) when the sun is glaring on the water. A very favourable time is just as it is getting dusk. I have had good sport harling when it was nearly dark." (W. B.)

"Sunrise and sunset for carp, bream and tench." (H. T. S.)

II. HEAT

Direct and indirect influence of heat.

"Extremes of temperature," writes Mr. Bagot, "are bad; great heat and a miserably chilly day equally so."

In the few remaining pages of this chapter on the connection between the sun and fishing we must consider some evidence of the effects, prejudicial or otherwise, of high temperatures. The part played by low temperatures, with the outward symbols of frost and snow, is discussed in Chapter III.

Excessive drought a bar to fishing.

The influence of a high temperature may be threefold. It may, and generally does, produce a hatch of insect food. It may either stimulate or deaden—opinions are divided on the matter—the appetites of the fish. Lastly, it may, in that excess which, combined with a low rain-fall, means drought, put a stop to fishing operations altogether. This last result is less familiar in temperate lands than in some hotter latitudes, where the fisher-man, in common with every one else, is more the sport of the sun than he would be in England. The converse of this is seen in colder countries, where, by ice instead of by drought, a similar veto is put on fishing by the other climatic ex-treme. It is in India more particularly Case of India that the angler is keenly sensitive to these changes. There, the hot weather, rains, and cold weather follow one another in a monotonous succession year after year, and with a precision unknown in the English climate, the keynote of which is constant surprise, mostly disagree-able, for those who take their plea-sure out of doors. In some districts of that country the mahseer-fisherman has to watch his opportunities very closely after the falling of the rivers at the end of the rains, for, though he has his best time when the water clears, it may so rapidly dry up that, after being in order for fishing for a week or two, it again dwindles to a series of isolated pools full of fish that are as adamant to all the angler's overtures.

Although the sun's heat means less to every one in northern Europe than in southern Asia, the influence of temperature on fish and fishing is by no means to be ignored, and some fishermen indeed consider it of first importance. It is on lake-trout that its effect is perhaps most noticeable. Writing of such, with reference to the Orkney lochs, Mr. Sutherland Graeme says :—

Trout in lakes.

" Loch-trout will not take if the water is too warm, but I cannot say that I have ever by thermometer tested the temperature at which they cease to rise. If there is a period of great heat, such as I have only known twice in Orkney, the fish in my shallow lochs just lie gasping

with their heads on the reeds at the edge
of the loch. They can then be taken out
by hundreds with the hand—fine fish
too. I now dam up the loch in early
summer, so that the increased volume of
water keeps the loch cool and fishable.
Temperature will, I feel certain, guide
investigators to lots of new knowledge. I
am sure, for instance, that it is simply a
question of shoals of herrings swimming
about to try and find the exact temperature they want to spawn in. When found,
they stay and spawn."

Another interesting communication on
the subject of the manner in which
temperature affects trout in lakes reaches
me from Mr. Munro Edwards, and is as
follows :—

"Cold weather puts the trout down.
Therefore I have never liked an east wind
when fishing a lake for trout, regarding south, or south-west, with a warmer
temperature, as better. There are, it is
true, some mountain llyns in the locality,[1]

[1] Merionethshire.

which are considered only worth visiting when the wind blows from an easterly quarter, but this may merely be an accident of situation."

Loch Lomond.

The sun, as may be supposed, soon warms the water of shallow lochs, as a result of which the fisherman gets his trout early and in good condition. Loch Lomond is a case of a deep lake, and quantities of snow-water run into it from the hills around. This makes it a late loch, there being, as a rule, no rise of fly until well on in May. Mr. Russell refers to this as solely a matter of temperature. "It appears to me," he writes, "simply that the cold water retards the rise of fly and the warm hastens it, and you do not get trout unless there is a rise. I am informed on excellent authority that, curiously enough, the head-waters of the streams in southern Perthshire are usually best for trout, owing to the fact that the water at their source is warmer than after exposure to the atmosphere, and consequently there is more insect food."

Other opinions might be cited in sup- port of the importance of temperature in different kinds of fishing. Mr. Wheeley, writing chiefly of the Thames and Wey, considers it all-important. The late Lady Bridge, who had considerable experience of salmon, was of opinion that that fish move when the temperature is "just beginning to change." Mr. G. Ashley Dodd reads the thermometer and barometer together thus:—

"A warm afternoon, turning to a cold evening, puts salmon down completely on the Thurso and is bad anywhere. A sudden fall of the barometer (as it generally means a gale) sets salmon jumping wildly, throwing themselves sideways, when they do not notice fly much. A fall of rain is rather good for salmon. But for trout, and still more for grayling, I like a rising barometer."

"Salmon," writes Mr. Barrington, "will not take well in hot weather, but cold (unless when a frost first sets in) does not affect them in the same way."

Though all those who have contributed to this volume deprecate any attempt to lay down hard and fast rules, several regard it as peculiarly difficult to generalise on this question of the temperature most suitable for fishing.

Difficulty of general- ising.

Sir Henry Seton-Karr contrasts the successful spring salmon-fishing on the Dee and Thurso, with ice on the banks, as well as the autumn season on the Tweed under similar conditions, with the midsummer sport enjoyed on many a salmon-river in Ireland or in Norway. Mr. Gallichan is equally at a loss to formulate any rule, seeing that he has caught trout, after sunset in April, in an atmospheric temperature below 32°, and also, during July, in a temperature of 80° in the shade.

Hot weather favourable in the eastern counties ;

It seems that hot weather is more favourable to fishing in some districts than in others. In the eastern counties for instance, thanks perhaps to the tonic effects of a bracing climate, trout retain their appetite through the hottest summer.

"On a broiling July day," writes Mr. Hall of a small preserved trout-stream in Norfolk that he has fished for many years, "when fishing in any south country trout-stream would be out of the question, fish will rise madly, and are far more easily taken than at sunset. It is well known that trout are more easily approached under such conditions, but unfortunately they are not normally feeding then, except in the Mayfly season."

Mr. Bryden is among the most enthu-siastic advocates of hot-weather fishing as a result of some successes under such conditions. "In Norway," he writes, "I have found hot, settled weather good for trouting; indeed, I have known the heat so tropical, especially in June 1893, that for a spell we did most of our fishing between 7 and 12 P.M. . . . On a day of clear intense heat I once had one of the finest days with pike that I remember. It was on a large and ancient Warwick-shire reservoir, and we killed a brace of 8 lbs. each, within a minute or two one of

in Norway;

for pike in a reservoir;

the other, having hooked them simultaneously. We also took about six or eight others, running from 4 lbs. to 9 lbs.

for char in Loch Tay.

Char I have taken freely on one or two occasions in Loch Tay in August during fine, hot, settled weather."

Mahseer may sulk in hot weather.

With reference to mahseer, to which allusion was made in the Introduction in connection with Colonel Bairnsfather's ingenious "normal weather" theory, and which is generally regarded as feeding best in the ordinary hot, sunny weather of India, an exception must be made to even this rule. Lieut.-Colonel H. H. Godwin-Austen tells me that he has seen mahseer in the large pools of the Rajawrie Tawi rolling over and jumping out of water on a hot evening, but that no fly would tempt them.

Other fish lethargic.

"Hot sun and continuous still, dry weather," writes Major Wynn Eyton, "will heat up the water and make the trout sick and lethargic."

Mr. Gallichan is of opinion that the majority of coarse fish, with the possible exception of carp and bream, are sleepy on the hottest days between 11 A.M. and 6 P.M.

"I believe," writes Sir John Edwards-Moss, "that salmon are very much influenced by temperature. See how they lie in the stream in hot weather and right down at the still tails of the pools in very cold water. Also note how they will take a huge fly in very cold water and require a tiny one to move them in very hot weather."

Major Eyton thinks that trout "are more affected as to their appetites by temperature than by actual weather, and it does not seem that any hard and fast rule can be made in either case. For instance, a good many years ago I was fishing the River Bride (Co. Waterford). The first day (3rd April) it was snowing hard nearly all day, but I caught, with the artificial fly, twenty-seven brown trout, weighing 11 lbs. 3 oz.: flies, March Brown, Hare's Ear, and February Red. Next day, very fine and warm; no rise,

Importance of temperature of water being higher than temperature of air.

and only got three small fish with worm. The river rose about six inches in the night after snow and was slightly discoloured. In this case it seems pretty certain that on the first day the air was cold, but the water warm. On the second day the water was cold, owing to melted snow, but the air was warm."

This relation between the temperature of the water and that of the atmosphere is in all probability the determining factor far more than the absolute temperature of the water without reference to other conditions. This is suggested at any rate by several other statements in the correspondence on the subject. Thus, Mr. Sheringham notes that so long as the water is warmer than the air, hail and snow need not put an end to sport. Mr. Rolt says that, though the air be piercingly cold, yet, if the water be a few degrees higher, roach will bite well; but with the air warmer than the water little sport may be looked for. Mr. Wheeley explains the readiness with which roach feed late in the summer evenings by the fact that the temperature of the water is then higher than that of the air.

Lastly, to a similar condition may be attributed the result of a good day's trout fishing enjoyed by Prof. Burkitt on Loch Fewn, Sutherland, 9th Sept. 1905. "It was," he writes, "quite cold and raining hard for a good part of the time, but the water felt warm when you put your hand in."

CHAPTER II

OF RAIN AND INCIDENTALLY OF HAIL
AND SLEET

You must abear the smart, my boys,
Be it hail, or rain, or snow.

HUGHES.

Discomfort of fishing in rain—Mr. Senior catches grayling in bad weather—Rain bad for dry-fly fishing—Clouds, rain and hail: various effects of rain—(*a*) CLOUDS——"Michelmore's cloud"—(*b*) RAIN—Raindrops on the surface—Mr. Earl Hodgson's view—Rain good for salmon and for trout; also in lake-fishing—Experience of Mr. Sheild—A case on Loch Leven—Rain on the Berwickshire Blackadder—Weight or opinion adverse to heavy rain—Discoloration of the water—Fatal yellow flood—Moss-water prejudicial to sport—Bass in muddy water—Level of the Water in Floods—Rising water bad for salmon—Best level for salmon fishing—On the rivers of Leinster—On the Bandon River—On the Tweed—Different effects on salmon and trout—Lord Breadalbane's note on the Orchy—Lord Montagu of Beaulieu on sea-trout in tidal reaches—Thames trout—General effects of flood and drought on salmon and sea-trout—Sir Roper Lethbridge on Dartmoor trout—(*c*) HAIL AND SLEET—Hail no bar to sport—Alleged habit of mahseer—Mr.

102

Buxton dislikes hail—Others less hostile—Mr. Sheild prefers it for spring fishing—A curious experience on the Esk—Other opinions favourable to hail and sleet —Advantage of alternate sunshine and rain.

THERE is a school of sportsmen which regards an alleged preference for fishing in dirty weather as the stamp of true sportsmanship. "Alleged" rather than real, because such professions of indifference to climatic discomfort are probably as little sincere as the assurance of those who go on the sea for pleasure that they find no enjoyment in smooth weather. Here and there, no doubt, it might be possible to find a joyless temperament capable of preferring Nature in her uncouth moods, but the normal human being is for her smiles. *Discomfort of fishing in rain.*

It is not, however, from this point of view that the prospects of sport on a wet day will be discussed in the present chapter.

It is assumed that the fisherman is sufficiently protected, or otherwise indifferent, to start out in a downpour, or at any rate with the certainty of rain before the day is out, and to remain at his post in spite of it. What has to be determined is the manner in which such weather is likely to affect his chances.

In aggravated cases the discomfort is so depressing as to rob even an unexpected success of its pleasure. Mr. Senior thus graphically describes a comfortless, but not unproductive, September day on the Exe, below Dulverton :—

" The weather was all that one wanted it not to be. There were squalls that roared with hoarse voices and rainstorms that blurred the surface of the stream at frequent intervals. But I was a couple of miles from headquarters, fully equipped, before the outburst came, and I braced myself to the forlorn hope of fishing steadily, come weal or woe, upstream and homewards. I waded as near the left-hand fringe of bushes as I could for shelter, and, with a short line, cast a small red quill straight ahead, fishing it dry on the chance of rising a fish. There was no appearance of any rise, even in those occasional lulls in which the blast lay low to gather fury for the next onslaught. Every angler knows the monotonous effect of this when nothing happens. Your thoughts gradually go abroad, and you swish on mechanically. This I did for an hour, plodding up in the troubled current. Then something did happen. I was rudely recalled to the work of the moment by a hooked fish. It was a grayling too, not a silly youngster, not even a rash "shott," as we call the fish of that variety that has not yet spawned, though almost mature; but an honest pounder, that knew the ways of the world he swam in. Buffeted by the north-wester, drenched with the pelting rain, up and up I waded, dreeing my weird as best I might for two hours, keeping to my steady casting and to my one fly, and leaving the fish to settle the rest for themselves. A fish, caught here and there, was a grim surprise rather than a pleasure, and it was a distinct relief when I saw that the road-washings had left no choice but an abandonment of the game. Under the lee of a moist haystack, I got out of harness and counted out $5\frac{1}{2}$ brace of grayling and trout. It may be objected that by fishing downstream with wet flies I should probably have caught three times the quantity; but this was not so, for on the same day, higher upstream, two very good fishermen tried that orthodox method with very indifferent result, leaving me to insist on the reversal of the accepted rules as regards both weather and the floating fly, and to draw the moral of perseverance in the face of conditions to all appearance hopeless."

This disagreeable experience is of interest from more standpoints than one, for, as the Editor of the *Field* points out in the last sentence, it bears not only upon the impossibility of laying down the law in matters of fishing weather, but it likewise strikes at a sacred canon of the dry-fly fisherman, touching the hopelessness of that method for grayling in blustering weather.   Here is what Mr. Buxton says on the subject :—

"The dry-fly has a reputation to keep up, and apparently refuses to do execution on a wet day, when there is water on its back."   Indeed, the Postmaster-General, a recognised authority on this method, whimsically extends the same dislike of rain to the dry-fly trout, which, he writes, "does not like getting wet ; while on a rainy day it is more difficult to spot the rising fish and the fish not actually rising, but ready to take." *Rain bad for dry-fly fishing.*

Of moisture in the atmosphere there are five separate stages that may, each in its own fashion, affect the fisherman's chances of sport.   Of these, three only are dealt with in the present chapter, snow and fog being considered later. Clouds, rain and hail have, however, been taken together, not without some risk of the evidence overlapping, partieu-larly in the often close connection between hail and snow, but because some such division was found necessary, and these *Clouds, rain and hail: various effects of rain.*

three phenomena are, on the whole, more associated with certain seasons of the year than any of them with snow, which belongs more properly to the period of frost.

It is further necessary to subdivide the influence of rain on failure or success in fishing under, at any rate, three heads: (1) The patter of raindrops on the surface, which, either by concealing the tackle, or, as some believe, by oxygenation, often brings a rise; (2) the discoloration of the water in flood-time, which necessarily hides the natural food supplies, and sometimes also the angler's lure, from those fish which hunt their prey by sight; and (3) the level of the river, a most important factor in salmon fishing, the significance of which, though perfectly appreciated, is but partially understood. It will be seen from these preliminary divisions of the subject that the conditions discussed in the present chapter are perhaps more complex in their origin and effect than those dealt with in any other.

(a) CLOUDS

Clouds, as the embryonic stage of rain, claim precedence, and only one communication of importance has reached me on the subject. The indirect effect of clouds, in diminishing the illumination of the background and thereby affecting the fly-fisher's sport on dull days, may be regarded as the converse of sunshine, and as such was incidentally considered under the head of LIGHT in the last chapter. What has now briefly to be considered is the more subtle influence of certain clouds, which cannot, for reasons which will be apparent in the quotation which follows, be attributed to any mere effect of the light. Though these clouds may possibly modify the appearance of the fly, it is far more likely that they are symptomatic of some atmospheric condition, which makes the fish reluctant to feed. It seems inconceivable that the presence of a particular cloud on the sky-line should so affect these creatures as to give them a distaste for their food, yet this has for so many years been Mr. Michelmore's experience of those white wool-pack clouds of the Devonshire moorland and Teign valley, that his angling friends have come to associate clouds of this description with his name. Here is his own account of the matter :—

"When there is a sign of one of these clouds about, I always find it impossible to move a decent trout. They usually appear on a bright, showery day, but I have known them to be about on a fine day after a night's rain when every condition appeared to be perfect for sport. I do not think that the lack of sport is due to their brightness, because the ordinary white clouds are equally bright. When they are about, trout will not rise even to a dry-fly, which they will do on the brightest and hottest summer day, if these particular clouds are not in evidence. I have known them in the sky from nine to twelve, and have not moved a fish. Other clouds have covered them from twelve to one, during which time I have had good sport. Then they have reappeared, and I have done nothing for the rest of the day. For the last twenty years, at any rate, I have had these clouds under very careful observation, and I have never had anything approaching decent sport when they have been visible."

This baneful cloud, so often Mr. Michelmore's undoing, is, I venture to think, the greatest mystery of all the many puzzling weather influences contributed by correspondents. In a general way, Mr. Dodd, as quoted in the last chapter, prefers bright sunshine to white clouds, but no similar specific accusation is elsewhere brought against a particular recurring cloud like that discovered by Mr. Michelmore. Mr. Horace Hutchinson's admission of "bright, white, hummocky clouds in a clear sky" as one of the only two atmospheric conditions fatal to success in trout fishing was referred to on an earlier page.

(b) Rain

(1) *Rain-drops on the Surface*

There are two theories touching the effect of a fall of rain on the surface of water, particularly of a lake unruffled by wind, and both of these, while attributing it to different causes, regard it favourably. In a few cases, it is true, as that of the half-bred Loch Levens in the artificial loch previously referred to by Mr. Black, rain seems to have no effect whatever, but this is exceptional. To some extent, too, so experienced a fisherman as Mr. Earl Hodgson regards rain as powerless to affect the chance of sport or to influence the mood of trout. "If," he writes, "they are rising, it does not make them cease to rise."

The more general view, however, is that a not too heavy downpour favours sport. This is explained by the majority of fishermen as the beneficial effect of rain-drops ruffling the surface in the absence of a breeze, a result peculiarly favourable on the smooth surface of still water, though advantageous even in running water. Thereby, it is argued, the fisherman's hook, and particularly the glint of his gut, is hidden from the fish. The other interpretation of the success which often follows a shower, preferred by Mr. Sheild, Dr. Bright, and one or two more correspondents, is that the appetites of the fish are stimulated by oxygenation. Whatever the cause, rain often brings luck to both salmon- and trout-fishermen, and the following are among the opinions in favour of it.

" Rain, if it is real rain (not mist), snow, and even hail I think favourable for salmon until the water has begun to rise perceptibly, say more than an inch or two. A shower of rain, with a puff from a dark cloud, on a sunny day I call a great opportunity with a Thunder-and-lightning ' fly '." (J. E.-M.)

Rain good for salmon

" I have seen salmon caught in heavy rain with a rising water." (J. F.)

" I do not think a shower has a bad

8

effect (on the Aberdeenshire Dee), but salmon never take well if the rain is likely to produce a rise in the water." (R. T. C.)

The foregoing three opinions also bear, it will be noticed, on the question of the level of the water, which is discussed at the end of the chapter.

" Salmon will take in rain, but not when heavy downpours are coming." (C. G. B.)

" In the Torridon (Ross-shire), the coarser the weather, the better the fishing, so long as there is not wind enough to blow the fly out of the water. The best rises frequently occur when there is a sharp patter of rain on the surface." (G. C.)

" Salmon often take well during rain, especially if the water is clear and there is no breeze to ruffle the surface." (J. C. D.)

and for trout; Trout - fishermen also favour rain, at any rate in moderation and sometimes even in abundance, as the following quotations illustrate:—

" Rain often (in Norway and Lapland)

starts a rise of brown trout, which will continue after the rain has stopped." (H. B. B.)

"In Banffshire rivers, small trout cease to take the fly in rain, but large trout are more readily caught during rain than at any other time." (J. C.)

It is, as might be expected, on the still surface of lakes that, in the absence of wind, the patter of rain exercises its beneficial influence appreciably.

"In some lakes, specially Talyllyn, trout rise best after rain, but never so well before a storm." (C. E. M. E.) *also in lake-fishing.*

"White and brown trout take well in some of the lakes in Co. Mayo during hard rain." (T. D.)

"For lake-fishing in Donegal, rain, hanging overhead, is bad, but light showers are good, and fish sometimes rise well during, and just after, heavy rain on a hot, close day." (W. E.-J.)

Among other experiences of good lake-fishing during rain, Sir Thomas Esmonde recalls killing over three dozen brown and sea-trout in very heavy rain during a couple of hours' fishing on Lake Devorgana, near Waterville, Co. Kerry; and Mr. Bryden remembers, as far back as 1874, a day of torrential rain on Loch Tummel, when he and a friend made a fine bag of trout.

Experience of Mr. Sheild.

Perhaps, however, the most remarkable experience of lake-fishing in rain is that communicated by Mr. Marmaduke Sheild as an experience of his own on Lake Beoraik, Inverness-shire. He relates it as follows :—

"When the water is strongly dimpled by heavy rain, the fish may temporarily go mad, and phenomenal baskets may then be made. I have experienced this in Loch Leven and elsewhere. An extraordinary instance is as follows. Many years ago, one hot August day, I was staying at Meoble Forest, Inverness-shire, and as the day was hot and sultry, and seemed hopeless for fishing, I determined to accompany the shepherds in their large boat to see them collect the sheep. We rowed up a lake (Beoraik) about three miles long and terminating in a large sandy bay, into which several streams flowed. I had taken the precaution to bring a fly-rod, net, and tackle. Early in the afternoon a desperately heavy storm came on. There was no wind, but the surface of the lake was splashed and churned by heavy thunder-rain. Seeing some fish move, I got into the boat and began to cast. Instantly two trout were hooked at once. The gear was strong and the flies large, as was the custom in those days and localities, and the fish got short shrift. For upwards of two hours, while the heavy rain lasted, I killed trout at every cast. I had no one to manage the heavy boat, which I allowed to drift aimlessly about the bay. It was impossible to go wrong. When the rain ceased, and the sun came out again intensely hot, the fish ceased rising with absolute suddenness. A large creel was filled, and strings of fish were made up by the shepherds from those thrown into a pool of water in the boat. The catch was never weighed or counted, but all the gillies declared that they had never seen a take like it made with the rod. Certainly, it exceeded anything else I have done before or since. Another remarkable fact was the unusual size of the fish, which ran two to the pound, with several of as much as two pounds, and this in a lake where trout of the 'herring' size are the rule. A friend of mine had a similar experience in Loch Leven, but in this case, the fish being large and the tackle fine, he lost many in his eagerness to profit by the rise. I attribute this extraordinary activity of the fish entirely to oxygenation of the water."

A case on Loch Leven.

A somewhat similar experience once befell Mr. Noble on the Berwickshire Blackadder. These are his words :—

Rain on the Berwickshire Blackadder.

" Some few years ago, I was fishing with a companion in the Berwickshire Blackadder. We started that morning in clear sunshine. Then, about noon, a soft, drizzling, warm rain began to fall and lasted all day. In my whole experience I never knew a rise of trout last so long. They were on the move for six hours. I started fishing down, but without success. I fished across, with the same result. So I fished up, with a short line, and found that the fish took freely just as the flies left the water. Between us, we had 70 trout weighing 21½ lbs."

Of heavy rain, it is the occasional experiences that are favourable. Thus, Mr. Sheringham caught his largest trout of 1905 in a drenching downpour. Yet even he prefers the effects of rain to its actual continuance. The majority of correspondents are against heavy rain, as for instance :—

"Heavy rain stops all rising in the Upper Tawe (Carmarthen), but a drizzle has little or no effect." (W. W. F.) Weight of opinion adverse to heavy rain.

"In trout fishing, heavy, cold rain is an abomination, but in a light, warm rain I have known the biggest baskets made." (G.)

"When a heavy fall of rain is impending, the trout know it beforehand and are slack in feeding." (St. V. B.)

"For loch-trout in Orkney, it is no use fishing in heavy rain. Owing, I suppose, to countless rain-drops, fish do not see the fly." (A. M. S. G.)

In this connection, General O'Callaghan mentions that, fishing with minnow on one occasion in the Till (Northumberland), he caught a fish about 5 A.M., and then, from 9.30 A.M., fished with fly in the rain, which commenced to fall soon after his first success, without touching another fish until about 3 P.M. In the two hours that followed, he landed 18 lbs. of trout, not one under $\frac{3}{4}$ lb., and then had to catch a train. Mr. Gallichan writes that he has found rainy weather favour bait-fishing for coarse fish, but not in a low temperature. "In some waters," he says, "trout will take the fly during rather heavy rain, though seldom during a drenching downpour. But in certain rivers, light rain seems to put trout down while it is falling. Generally speaking, light showers favour the angler. Very wet seasons, especially if the weather is cold, do not prove highly successful as a rule. Fish are often lively just before heavy rain, though at times threatening rain seems to have the same effect as an approaching thunderstorm. Between the showers, if the temperature is not cold, most fish appear to be in quest of food. But experience shows that the influence of rain is very contradictory, and it seems almost impossible to affirm positively concerning the result."

(2) *Discoloration of the Water*

Of the colours produced in the water by sky-reflections, something was said in the last chapter. Very different, in origin and effect, is the thickening of the water by mud or peat-stain as the result of floods. As a rule, this hinders fly-fishing, but gives the best sport with worm and other baits. Yet the fly does well again as soon as the water clears, which it does rapidly in chalk-streams, where both trout and grayling take the fly at once. In some streams, too, there are, owing to the currents, patches of clear water outside the discoloured area, where fish may be caught. "I have," writes Colonel Davies-Cooke, in allusion to this condition, "known about half of a stream as thick as soup, the rest scarcely coloured."

Fatal yellow flood. One of the worst forms of discoloration by a spate is that yellow flood, fortunately rare in dry-fly streams, but only too familiar in some parts of the country. General O'Callaghan remembers two occasions on which the dreaded apparition of this yellow stain drove him from water otherwise in perfect order. Neither time did he receive any warning of the impending change, for the rain that was the cause of it had fallen far away in the hills and not in the low country where he was fishing.

Moss-water prejudicial to sport. "The moss-water from the hills," writes Colonel M'Inroy, "seems to make the fish sulky when the water is thereby rendered thick, but when it settles, and the water (in the North Esk) is left clear, though brown, we get fish when they are there." Colonel M'Inroy here distinguishes between a condition of turbid opaqueness and one in which, though of abnormal colour, the water remains translucent. The distinction is familiar to most fishermen.

There is a muddy condition of the estuary water of the Teign, caused by heavy rain draining off Dartmoor, which gives the water the appearance of pea-soup. At such times, not a bass is to be caught until, at any rate, a high tide has cleared the river with pure sea-water. This rule I have, during six summers in succession spent on that estuary in daily pursuit of bass, found practically without exception. Whether the bass remain in the river and are merely unable to see the live sand-eel used as bait, or whether, with the water so foul, these estuarine fish move out over the bar until it clears again, we do not know.

Bass in muddy water.

(3) *Level of the Water in Floods*

The causes and effects of discoloration of a river are approximately easy to trace. The results of a high or low level of the water are equally recognised, but are more difficult to explain. Certain conditions are admitted as corresponding on a particular river with good or bad sport. These vary, however, in different localities, and as the two are closely associated, it is not always easy to discuss them apart from the colour of the water. All that can here be offered is an indication of general principles.

Rising water
ɔad for
salmon.

Sir John Edwards-Moss and Colonel Caldwell have already been quoted in the present chapter to the effect that a rise in the water may be bad for salmon, and Sir James Fergusson, on the other hand, as having had experience of good sport under such conditions. Sir Henry Pottinger writes thus on the subject of salmon in rising water :—

"My experience teaches me that

when, owing to excess of rain, the water begins to rise and continues rising, even although it be scarcely discoloured, sport with the fly is, for the time being, at an end. This is especially the case with salmon."

Mr. Sheild pleads for latitude in estimating such conditions as favourable, or otherwise, to the salmon-fisherman. "As regards salmon," he writes, "many years of experience have taught me this broad truth. The caprice of both salmon and sea-trout is quite inexplicable, and, while knowing the conditions which suit them well, the fisherman need never despair of catching a fish in most unfavourable weather. I have always looked upon a falling and clearing water, after a heavy spate, as the most favourable condition for salmon, and an exactly opposite condition is equally likely, that is to say, the first flow of flood-water into a well-stocked pool. The salmon crowd to the head, and take with avidity on the first run of the flood-water. I have had many experiences of this."

Best level for salmon fishing.

After saying that salmon often take a fly best in a normal spate following a prolonged period of drought, and with the river rising slowly, Mr. Munro Edwards continues : "Constant spates, keeping the fish, as it were, on the move, render them restless, very seldom inclined to rise to a fly, or take any bait at all. On the other hand, if, after a spate, the river falls rapidly, more rain is portended, especially if the water retains a dark, peaty hue. Under such conditions I have seldom had much sport with either salmon or sewin. On the Mawddach this is especially noticeable. Clearer water after a heavy spate often means fine weather to follow, and if the river falls gradually, salmon and sewin are more eager for the fly than if the river fell rapidly and retained its dark, peaty colour. . . . Sewin will take a bait of worms more readily than salmon or grilse when the river rises gradually in flood. On the other hand, if the rise of water be sudden and heavy, neither salmon nor sewin will take at all. . . . Dull,

SALMON JUMPING THE FALLS

warm, rainy weather is bad for fishing, whereas cold, rough, rainy weather means a good day's sport on the Mawddach. It cannot be too rough. . . . There is no doubt that the rapid fall of water in our Welsh streams after a spate, brought about by the extensive drainage of the watersheds, influences to a great extent the habits of our *Salmonidæ*. This rapid fall in the height of the water causes fish to settle down at the bottom of the pools, and under rocks in deep water, much sooner than formerly. This fact may be one of the reasons why salmon often take a fly much more eagerly when at the tail of a pool than when the river has fallen and the fish have ascended into the deeper and rockier parts of the pools.'

With regard to the best conditions for salmon fishing in the rivers of the Province of Leinster, Colonel St. Leger Moore writes as follows :— On the rivers of Leinster.

"The best weather conditions for catching fish in the rivers here are when the wind is south or west and rain begins to fall just before a flood. One is almost certain to get fish then, however bad the fishing may have been before. Even when the water has risen a good deal, and is colouring, one has a good chance. I find, however, that it is quite hopeless when the flood is high and the water discoloured, and I have in vain tried flies, large and small, prawn, minnow, worm, etc. It is also almost impossible to catch fish for some twelve hours when the river begins to fall."

On the Bandon River.

"The salmon of the Bandon River are," writes Mr. Conner, "supposed not to take when rain is coming on, or when the river is rising, but this is not at all a certain rule, as on the 17th September last I killed five, several of them during rain, and on two occasions that summer I killed fish in rising water."

On the Tweed.

It is also well known that rising water is against fishing on the Tweed, and Mr. Sheild confirms this. "A high flood," he writes, "dirty and foul, is bad for salmon. But height of water, provided it be *falling*

and *clearing*, is no bar, and I have taken
salmon in the Tweed, literally in the
water over grass by the side of the
stream, using a very large and gaudy fly."

Sir Henry Seton-Karr notes that rain, Different
by increasing the volume of water and effects on
discolouring it, affects trout less than trout.
salmon, for the former are on the prowl
for food, whereas the latter, when not running, lie at the bottom of the river and rise
only occasionally at the fly. When the
river is really rising in flood, salmon will
not look at a fly, as all their energies are
concentrated on getting up to the higher
reaches. "Yet," he concludes, "there is
an exception even to this rule, since
salmon will often rise greedily in the
first stir of a flood when the fresh water
first reaches them. . . . A friend of mine
on one occasion killed three fish in rapid
succession under such circumstances, and
then the flood came in fuller volume, and
the rise at once ceased. Before the water
began to stir, he could not rise a fish. I
once killed two good fish on the Dee in

this first half-hour of a flood, after fishing the two days previous without a rise. Again, the depth of water is all-important in influencing a salmon's rise. . . . The fish do not lie at all in certain throws, unless the depth of water suits them. None of these considerations apply in the case of trout."

Lord Breadal-bane's note on the Orchy. It is of the first importance to ascertain from local information the precise degree of spate in which any particular river, or pool of a river, is likely to give the fisherman of its best. Of the Orchy, for instance, which I fished unsuccessfully in a moderate height of water during the autumn of 1905, Lord Breadalbane writes: "The Orchy has its source in Loch Tulla, of course small streams falling into it, but its course on the main body of the water comes from the loch, and therefore it does not come down coloured like many streams, for instance the Tweed, which, in high spate, is often unfishable on account of its colour. The Orchy does not fish well when very small.

I have noticed that the best sport is obtained when the river is not in great flood, but what one might term a 'middling-size spate.'"

Lord Montagu of Beaulieu suggests a rule for sea-trout in tidal reaches. The influence of the tides causes another form of rise and fall in the lower reaches of rivers debouching on the sea, and of sea-trout in such conditions his long experience has taught him that these fish take best on the rising tide in those waters which are subject to rise and fall.

Most fish appear to be put off the feed by a rapid rise in the water, but for Thames trout Mr. Wheeley regards a swift and sudden rise as a good condition, *if with no extra colour in the water.* This reservation he underlines.

Generally speaking, it is obvious that a period of drought on a salmon-river means abundance of fish for the nets working down in the estuary, where fish congregate in their hundreds, waiting for the first favourable chance to ascend, but

Lord Montagu of Beaulieu on sea-trout in tidal reaches

Thames tront.

General effects of flood and drought on salmon and sea-trout.

a corresponding dearth of fish for the rods above. On a trout-stream, heavy rain discolours the water, and, by washing down abundance of worms and grubs, gives the bait-fisher his opportunity.

Sir Roper Lethbridge on Dartmoor trout.

In some rivers, indeed, it looks as if the trout were capable of anticipating this coming bounty, and in consequence declining the gifts of the Greeks. As Sir Roper Lethbridge reminds me, when the water of the streams running off Dartmoor and Exmoor begins to rise rapidly, the trout refuse to follow their example. A fall of rain may have one more result that has not been previously taken into account. It may, and generally does, raise the temperature of the water, even to the extent of bringing out a hatch of fly. This puts the Stewart tackle out of court and reinstates the fly-book.

(c) Hail and Sleet

As has been already pointed out, these conditions are with difficulty separated in a discussion of this kind from snow, so that to some extent the reader will do well, as regards the rest of the evidence in this chapter, to read it, by cross-reference, in conjunction with much of that given in the next. At the same time, hail is so common an accompaniment of sport at a season when we have no snow, that this is thought the most satisfactory division.

Lord Wolverton and some others regard hail showers with indifference as neither good nor bad for fishing. Mr. Sheringham offers the interesting suggestion, as the result of observation, that hail is no bar to sport so long as the temperature of the water remains higher than that of the air. Such, at any rate, was the case when, in April 1905, he caught a 2 lb. trout—a good fish for the water, during a sharp hailstorm. *Hail no bar to sport.*

The patter of hailstones on the surface of the water seems to have a strange fascination for the mahseer. General Morton, Colonel Bairnsfather and other *Alleged habit of mahseer.*

correspondents with experience of Indian
fishing refer to a habit which, according
to native report, the mahseer has of rising
to the surface and swallowing the hailstones, even, it is said, to the extent of
dying of a surfeit of this cold food.
General Morton, without going so far
as to confirm the native belief, admits
that he has seen mahseer show themselves very freely during showers of hail,
so that, at any rate, whether they eat it
or not, it does not put them down.
Indeed, Colonel Deane has made a good
bag of them, with fly or fly-spoon, during
a heavy storm of rain and hail.

Mr. Buxton
dislikes hail.

Mr. Buxton, whose fancy for dry
weather as well as dry-fly has already
been illustrated, dislikes hail, and not
without good cause, as the following
reminiscence will show :—

"On the Kennet, some time ago, in
early June, I was catching fish freely,
when suddenly a heavy hailstorm came
on, churning up the water; and though
the rise of the fly was unaffected, not a

fish would move until the storm was well over. I am inclined to think that a hailstorm frightens the fish and chills them."

'Mr. Munro Edwards has more agree- Others less hostile. able memories of trout in hailstorms. " I have," he writes, "done well with trout during a hailstorm. Perhaps the hailstones are mistaken by the trout for some sort of food." Here, though without any suggestion that they actually eat the stones, is an analogous case to that of the mahseer. Sir Richard Bulkeley has known good days in snow and hail on spring salmon-rivers, though he considers that they may spoil sport with trout.

" In early spring - fishing for trout," Mr. Sheild prefers it for spring fishing. writes Mr. Sheild, " a fall of rain, hail, or even snow will often cause trout temporarily to rise. A heavy fall of hail is often followed by a gleam of sun, and the temperature of the air is raised. A small hatch of duns or March Browns frequently at once ensues and puts the trout on the feed. I also incline to the belief that the disturbance of the water may temporarily increase oxygenation. Be this as it may, I have for years, when fishing in the spring in the Tweed or Border streams, always looked upon a hailstorm as a good omen, and have never failed to fish *during the fall.*

"In April 1905 I was fishing in the Eamont (Cumberland), and the day was as bad and as unpropitious as it could be : dull, leaden clouds, a bitter N.E. wind, and not a trace of insect life visible. There had been a frost in the morning. Up to 12 o'clock I had taken only a few under-sized trout, which were returned. About 12.30 a heavy storm of hail and sleet broke on the river. This had not lasted ten minutes before I noticed a few large light-coloured March Browns float-ing down, and a few scattered rises were also evident. In a brief space of time I took ten good-sized trout, though I had fished the same water unavailingly before. The flies were fished wet and allowed to sink very deep. The storm was so heavy that a pile of hail and snow rested on my creel, and several other anglers, who were out and who sought shelter, scarcely got a fish between them. Such instances are probably in the experience of most practical fishermen."

An experience, probably in some respects unique, which befell Mr. Noble, may here, though it also involves the influence of conditions dealt with in later chapters, be cited. He tells it thus :—

"On one occasion, thirty-three years ago, my father, an old Tweedside fisher, and myself were fishing the Esk. Our sport had been nil; clear sunshine and great heat. Then came a slight, warm shower of rain, and then a thunderstorm, which, having lasted for some time, turned to hail and snow. We had arrived at a spot now occupied by Gladhouse Reservoir, the Edinburgh water-supply. The trout were on the move, and as quickly as my father cast his line he had trout. In ten minutes or so we

A curious experience on the Esk.

had three dozen. When the snow and hail came, all was still. I have fished for thirty-six years and I never saw anything else like it."

Others less hostile.

Mr. J. S. Tulloch informs me that, in Shetland, he has made an excellent basket of trout in May, fishing with fly, during, and immediately after, sleet; and Mr. Russell also remembers catching trout freely with fly during hail showers.

Lord Suffolk informs me that Mr. Barker, who owns the Fairford water on the Coln, has killed trout between hail-storms, and that his own keeper, W. Davidson, has, in March, killed trout in the Don under similar conditions. Lord Montagu likewise recalls catching two sea-trout, weighing nearly 12 lbs., "in the middle of a most violent hailstorm, the hail being so fierce that I was unable to see a double-hooked Jock Scott drop on the water, yet the fish seemed to be more lively than ever during the storm."

It will be remembered that several correspondents expressed themselves (see

Chapter I.) in favour of alternate dull sky and gleams of sun; and that veteran sportsman, Sir Henry Pottinger, with characteristic reluctance to dogmatise, suggests the broader application of a similar rule in respect of rain.

"In dry, hot weather," he writes, "a heavy shower, without thunder, will often bring trout up and set them feeding briskly, and, on the other hand, a gleam of sunshine, occurring on a dull, depressing day, will have an exactly similar effect. Ideal 'fishermen's weather,' therefore, would seem to consist in a happy alternation of blue skies with sunshine and clouds with rain. But I repeat that the experience of anglers is so infinitely varied—inasmuch as success is often attained under conditions apparently the most adverse, while failure as often results under those that seem most favourable — that any attempt to be dogmatic on the subject would be absurd."

CHAPTER III

OF FROST AND SNOW

First it blew,
Then it snew,
Then it thew.

I. FROST: Advantages of frost and sunshine—Good sport in frosty weather—The passing of the frost—Seasonable cold not prejudicial — Frost good for grayling—Opinions hostile to frosty weather—Temperature and coarse fish—Mr. Matthews on the effects of frost.

II. SNOW: Snow not a bar to sport—Mr. J. J. Hardy's experience on the Aln—In Norway and Lapland—Curious experience of Sir Douglas Brooke—Other instances of good sport in snowstorms—Case of the Thames trout—Snow good for salmon fishing—A snowstorm on the Slaney.

III. SNOW-BROTH: Cases of sport with melted snow in the water—Snow-broth in Canada and Norway—Evidence hostile to snow-broth—Touching mahseer fishing.

WE have so far considered conditions which belong rather to spring and summer than to any colder season of the year. Yet the angling enthusiasm

140

burns brightly through the winter days, and we must now review some of the ways in which frost and snow may affect the prospects of sport. Something was incidentally said in Chapter I. of the effect of a low temperature on fishing, chiefly in explanation of the converse results of a high temperature. In Chapter II., also, it was found impracticable to omit all consideration of snow when dealing with rain and hail. A fuller discussion has, however, been left for the present chapter.

I. Frost

The very low temperature which paints the riverside landscape white with frost is usually regarded as disastrous to fishing. Of a truth, there are other forms of sport more suitable under such conditions. Nevertheless, some anglers actually welcome a frost. The late Lady Bridge wrote me that she always rose, and often landed, salmon when white

Advantages of frost and sunshine.

frost was all over the ground in the morning, even with the water low and the sky cloudless. Indeed, a combination of bright sunshine and frosty weather would seem to be very favourable to salmon fishing. Sir John Edwards-Moss considers that bright sunshine even improves the fisherman's chances during a frost. "One does not," he adds, "often get a fresh fish before mid-day in frosty weather early in the year, though one gets worried by kelts. It looks as if the fresh fish wait till the water is 'aired' before rising."

Of good sport with both salmon and trout in a hard frost, and particularly later in the day after a night of frost, my correspondence contains so many evidences that some selection is called for, since the mere compatibility of the two seems too evident to need the weight of testimony.

Good sport in frosty weather.

Sir Herbert Maxwell remembers taking a yellow trout on a salmon - fly in the Thurso, in February, "fishing in a narrow run between solid ice-sheets six

inches thick." General Dalton writes:
"In a loch I have had fine sport with
salmon in snowstorms and frost, when my
line was freezing so hard that it would
scarcely run through the rings, but this
was 'harling' and not casting. After a
frosty night," he adds, "salmon seldom rise
early." Mr. Barrington also recollects
catching salmon when the top-ring of the
rod had to be warmed to prevent its being
choked with ice. Mr. Conner writes that,
after an October frost, salmon may be
killed in the Bandon River, in low water,
with the shrimp and also, he thinks, with
the fly. In spring, on the other hand,
he does not think fish take well after frost.

As has been said above, whatever may
be the opinion of anglers as to sport
during actual frost, there seems no doubt
that the chances are good when it is
going, as, for instance, in the afternoon
of a mild day following a hard frost
overnight. Thus, Lord Granby is of
opinion that it is useless to go after
trout "until any frost there may have

The passing
of the frost

been has been dispelled by the mid-day sun." Lord Wolverton regards frost in early morning, say up to about 11 A.M., as excellent, but he considers that it is against sport when it lasts all day.

"I am never," writes Colonel St. Leger Moore of the rivers of Leinster, "able to kill fish when the frost is on the ground, and things are white with it, or in a thick, frosty fog ; but I have killed fish when the frost was going."

"Salmon," writes Colonel Caldwell, "do not take well in the morning till any hoar-frost on the grass has melted.'

Seasonable cold not prejudicial.

It will have been noted just above that one correspondent referred to spring frosts as not conducive to sport. Mr. Earl Hodgson, on the other hand, regards these seasonable frosts in the early part of the year as by no means unfavourable to sport. Only unseasonable cold, he says, acts adversely to the fisherman's interests. "Early in spring,' he writes, "when frost occurs, it is usually among the conditions which are favourable, and it does not often occur later in the season. Sometimes, although there is no actual frost, the temperature is abnormally low in summer and in autumn. When that happens, sport is poor; but I think that the prominent condition of the atmosphere is only a symptom of the cause. It may be that the trout are down because flies are not up." Other correspondents, indeed, regard frost as a help in spring salmon-fishing. Mr. Marston gives a good reason for holding this opinion. After a frosty night a river may have run down to the right height for the best pools, owing to the frost having arrested the flow of water from the burns.

Of all the *Salmonidæ*, the grayling Frost good alone is generally regarded as feeding for grayling. better after a frost. Mr. Gallichan, alone among those who refer to this fish, does not favour frosty weather, but has found that his best days with grayling in November and December have been "mild, with a little sunlight at noon."

10

Yet some of the biggest bags of grayling on record in Yorkshire rivers have been made in bright, dry, frosty weather. Mr. Senior, a grayling enthusiast, is most hopeful on a morning of sunshine and stillness after a white frost. Mr. Sheringham made his best bag of grayling for 1904 on a December day, when it was freezing slightly the whole time he was out. Mr. Rolt, a recognised authority on this fish, also considers an overnight frost and a dull day, with occasional sunshine and no wind, to follow, ideal conditions for sport. "In frosty weather," he adds, "when the wet-fly has frozen into a tiny mass of ice on being taken out of the water for a few moments, grayling have taken freely."

Opinions hostile to frosty weather. Many salmon- and trout-fishermen oppose frost unconditionally. Mr. Munro Edwards has never enjoyed much sport with trout after a white frost in the morning. He considers that it makes both salmon and sewin "dour." He notes, writing chiefly of North Wales, that a white frost is often followed by a change in the weather.   Sir Douglas Brooke has on his grouse mountain a small loch absolutely crammed with very small trout, but it is useless to fish for these after a night's frost.   Sir William Dalgleish describes frost as bad for salmon fishing in the Tay, and Captain Edgeworth-Johnstone condemns it for Donegal rivers generally.   Mr. Black says that it is fatal in the case of the Loch Levens in the artificial loch near Edinburgh referred to in previous chapters.   As for barbel, very few seem to be caught in the winter months at all.   Mr. Wheeley, who has fished steadily through many winters on the Thames and Wey, using leger-tackle for perch, roach, and chub, has never in his whole experience caught a winter barbel.   His best sport, on the contrary, with that fish has been in warm weather, after rain, with W. or S.W. wind.[1]   The

[1] The first recorded winter barbel were two, of small size, captured by bank anglers at Weybridge, February, 1906.   The weather at the time was mild, and the water was in flood.

Temperature and coarse fish.

bream is another warm - weather fish, and Mr. Wheeley remarks that, although the best time for bream fishing is during the calm, hot weather in September, these sometimes feed well on a mild day in February, so long as the water is not then too thick. Chub, on the other hand, feed well in frosty weather and clear water, and a slight frost sometimes makes pike more eager for the bait. "Roach and perch," writes Mr. Sheringham, "sometimes feed well in frost, but on the whole prefer open weather. On some waters, roach seem not to feed very well in winter; on others, it is the best season for them." Mr. Rolt has also found that, though the first sharp frost puts roach off the feed, they soon grow accustomed to the cold and then come readily to the bait.

Mr. Matthew on the effects of frost.

Mr. Matthews, who has had great experience of coarse fish in most kinds of weather, sends some interesting notes on the effects of frost. "I have fished," he writes, "in many sharp frosts, but it has

been the exception rather than the rule
to find fish feeding during the first day
or two of a frost. The sudden change
seems to make all fish, even pike, rather
torpid, but I have had some good sport
when the fish have accustomed themselves to the new conditions. One of
my best baskets of Thames roach was
made when the weather was so severe
that a robin perched on my rod for some
time, and my puntsman and I fed two
robins with bread-crust in the 'parlour'
of the punt. Hard frosts drive all kinds
of fish to take shelter under the roots
and bushes. I once caught some roach
through a hole in the ice in the Suffolk
Stour. The river was open in the channel,
but at the spot where I fished in the
slack stream there was a deep pool,
with ice an inch thick." Mr. Matthews
has often had good chub fishing with
the rod - rings choked with ice, and
he has found that fish bite ravenously
in frosty weather, but he thinks that
roach and other kinds of fish feed

slowly when the water strikes colder than the air.

As regards frost, then, we have seen that it is favourable to grayling fishing, and that, so long as it goes off during the morning, a frost overnight may benefit the salmon and trout fishing next day. In the case of some specified rivers and lakes, however, it seems fatal to sport, and its effect is not the same on all coarse fish, bream preferring warm weather, and barbel being rarely caught in cold.

II. SNOW

To some extent, snow is associated with frost, but it may be absent in the hardest frost, and, on the other hand, it may lie along the banks of the river with the temperature either above or below freezing-point. Again, there is a distinct condition, when snow melts into the river, known as "snow-broth," which will be considered separately. In many cases where a fall of snow is not fatal, or even prejudicial, to sport, this melted snow, thickening the water, puts almost all fish off the feed.

Though the conditions accompanying snow are more conducive to pleasure when shooting, those who are willing to face the cold and other discomfort often speak highly of the sport.   Colonel Broadfoot has caught trout in the Aberdeenshire Don in a snowstorm in May, and Mr. Smart, writing from Budleigh Salterton, has made good baskets in both the Exe and the Otter during a fall of snow in early spring.   Mr. Earl Hodgson considers that snow is not in itself adverse to sport, and says that it often falls amid atmospherical conditions favourable to the fisherman. Snow not a bar to sport.

One of the most striking cases of a good bag made in a heavy snowstorm in the spring fishing on the Aln is communicated by Mr. J. J. Hardy, as experienced a fisherman as any in the Border country.   He was fishing with his father at Broom Park, and they Mr. J. J. Hardy's experience on the Aln.

caught between them eight or ten dozen trout. "During the morning," he writes, "very few fish would rise, but in the afternoon we had a very severe thunderstorm with snow. During the snowstorm, while the flakes were falling thick on the water, the fish rose madly. It was a most curious incident and made a great impression on me at the time—the dense snowstorm wrapping everything in white, the stillness, the oppressive silence, and the two of us catching trout just as fast as we could cast, while our coats were white with clinging snow."

In Norway and Lapland.

Dr. Baker noticed during his fishing excursions in Norway and Lapland that the usual effect of a fall of snow was to put the small trout off the feed, but to bring the larger fish on. "Small fish," he writes, "go down at once. Big fish rise fairly. I got three brown trout, each over 2 lbs., in half an hour in a snowstorm. I had been getting half-pounders up to the time the storm came on, but they did not rise at all later."

"On the 30th March 1891," writes Curious experience of Sir Douglas Brooke. Sir Douglas Brooke, "the water was dead low. A very cold N.E. wind was blowing, and there were constant showers of hail and snow. I had to go to a small river (in Co. Fermanagh) some few miles away, to settle a dispute between two tenants, which had arisen over the river having slightly altered its course during the winter floods. I took a rod with me, more to give myself something to do as I walked up the river than in any expectation of catching fish. However, I had the best afternoon I ever had on that river, killing twenty-six fish. They rose freely and boldly to a March Brown, but there was no sign of any natural fly on the water."

Sir George Brown remembers, while Other mstances of good sport in snowstorms. fishing in Gloucestershire, on the little stream which runs through Stroud, meeting a man who had had an excellent day's sport the previous Friday during a severe snowstorm. Colonel Cornwallis West has caught trout in the Dee (near

Corwen, Merionethshire) in a snowstorm, with the wind in the east; and a friend of Mr. Noble once made a great basket of trout in the Haddingtonshire Tyne in spring in a snowstorm, with the sun trying to break through. Dr. William Murray writes that the Coquet and other Border streams often fish well in April in a partial fall of snow, "especially with glints of sunshine"; and Dr. George Murray sends the following experience of one of them: "I was fly-fishing early in the season on a small stream in Northumberland, on a day when the water was in good order, and there were heavy snowstorms at intervals. I remember well that the trout rose freely during each shower of snow and stopped at once when it was over."

"Snowstorms," writes Mr. Gallichan, "usually put trout down, though they will often rise well between snow showers in April. I have caught trout once or twice during a shower of snow, but this is exceptional."

A ROUGH DAY AND BOILING WATER

So far we have been taking evidence in respect of ordinary brown trout. As the season for that coveted and mysterious fish, the Thames trout, opens (as some consider, most appropriately) on the first of April, snow is, as might be expected, no unusual condition of the sport, nor, according to Mr. Gomm, who has had many successes with this fish, is it necessarily against good results. Among many interesting memories of Thames trout which he has given me, the following is well worth quoting :—

"I remember, some three or four seasons back, starting on the opening day. The water was in the worst possible condition—very thick and bank-high. There was no sun, and the day was cold and windy, the exact opposite of the recognised trout weather. I wore an overcoat, but was cold in spite of it. My boatman said that we had better stay at home, but I have not missed the First for years, and went as a matter of duty. About 2 o'clock it commenced to snow heavily, and I made for a sheltered hole known as the Tumbling Bay, Penton Hook, with little hope of seeing a fish. Within half an hour, I caught three Thames trout in splendid condition, $6\frac{1}{2}$, $5\frac{3}{4}$, and $4\frac{1}{2}$ lbs., and this in a blinding snowstorm."

Mr. Wheeley also mentions having killed this fish in both hail and snow, "one fish in a blinding snowstorm, others in blazing sun."

Snow good for salmon fishing.

Ordinary trout and Thames trout may, then, take well in snow. Salmon seem to be still more approachable under such conditions, and indeed a fall of snow seems positively favourable. Colonel M'Inroy writes of the upper waters of the North Esk: "In one pool I killed salmon in the same week in a snowstorm and in a thunderstorm. . . . In October 1881 I killed three salmon and a sea-trout in a short afternoon, hooking every one of them *during* snow squalls. *Between* the squalls, not one would look at me."

Mr. Bagot and Mr. Dodd are among

those correspondents who favour snow for
salmon fishing. Colonel St. Leger Moore
contributes the following strange experience of salmon in a snowstorm :—

"In March 1893 I went down to the A snowstorm
Slaney, which was high and coloured, and on the
Slaney.
as I was putting up my rod it began to
snow. The wind was in the north and
rather high, and the day was very cold.
I put on the casting-line and left it to soak
in the water while I took refuge under a
big rock. After half an hour or so, as it
was snowing worse than ever, I got tired
of sitting down, and thought that I would
try a few casts to warm me. I took up
the rod, let out a few yards of line, and
cast out towards a rock opposite. I had
only a very short line, but I saw a fish
come with a boil at the fly, found I was
in him, and killed him. Lower down
the pool I got another, and altogether I
took four clean-fish (besides three kelts,
which I returned) in one of the worst
snowstorms I ever was out in in this
country, and went home at 3 P.M."

It seems that it is not very common to catch salmon in Irish rivers during the falling of snow, for Mr. Conner thinks it worth mentioning that he knew a single case of a salmon taken with fly under such conditions in the Bandon in the month of March, about three years ago.

As regards sea-fishing, I do not think that a fall of snow affects ground-fish, and surface-fishing is for the most part over by that season. Snowy weather may, as Mr. Minchin reminds me, indirectly benefit the pier - fisherman by bringing the larger cod inshore. Whether they seek shallower, and therefore warmer, water, or come in pursuit of sprats, I am not sure.

III. SNOW-BROTH

We have seen the effects of snowstorms on fishing for trout and salmon. Until the snow has melted into the river, the fall does not appear to influence sport beyond what would be expected of a low temperature. A very heavy fall on a still lake would, and probably does, dimple the surface after the manner of rain or hail. When, however, the snow melts off the land, and the river is thickened with the product, which fishermen call "snow-broth," a very different result is noted. On the whole, and taking the weight of evidence from a variety of localities far apart, it may be regarded as fatal to sport, and a good catch with snow-broth in the water will be noted as an exception. Yet it is not unknown.

The late Lady Bridge caught a 43 lb. autumn salmon on the fly when the Spean was full of snow-water. In April 1881 Colonel St. Leger Moore made a great basket of trout on the Liffey " when the water was almost green from the melted snow coming off the mountains." In this case, it is probable that the melting snow had some distance to travel before reaching the spot at which he was fishing, rising in temperature or otherwise losing its deleterious properties. Mr. Champneys suggests a similar

Cases of good sport with melted snow in the water.

phenomenon in the following experience : " The best trout fishing I ever had—good sport, lasting for many days—was on a Scotch river in a succession of freshets caused by the snow melting during warm nights. It is clear that in this case the factor to be taken into account was the distance of the mountains, which held the snow, from the fishing-ground, taken in connection with the average depth and pace of the stream. In this instance, the length of run would measure some twelve to fifteen miles, a considerable portion of which would be over shallows, in which the water would rapidly become warmer. The question, in fact, is not whether snow or rain is the cause of the fresh, but merely one of temperature."

Snow-broth in Canada and Norway.

This last opinion of Mr. Champneys is not borne out by other correspondents, all of whom, save in the exceptional cases mentioned, recognise some mysterious hostile property in snow-broth, quite distinct from the mere operation of temperature. For instance, General

Dalton, pointing out the importance of snow-broth in Canada and in Norway, says that he has found that, while fresh water is absolutely necessary in the river, if sport is to be reckoned on, salmon take the fly better when the snow-water is run down, and the water of the river has had time to get warmed.

Mr. Rolt writes that snow-water be- Evidence hostile to snow-broth. numbs roach, "and to fish for them while snow-broth is in the river is a case of love's labour's lost. While there has been snow in the water, grayling have sometimes fed, while at others they have refused to do so." A possible explanation of this apparent contradiction is offered by Mr. Gallichan, whose experience of grayling in Derbyshire streams is that they do not go off the feed in snow-water so long as the temperature does not rise above freezing-point. As regards trout, Mr. Gallichan had it from a reliable professional fisherman in Wales that he had made a heavy catch with worm when snow was melting in the river. Mr.

Gawthorne, writing of the Avon at Salisbury, regards snow-broth as fatal to pike, and Mr. Wheeley has no better opinion of it in respect of roach. "I have," he writes with reference to this matter, "had good bags of roach, with snow actually falling, but when the snow has melted and run into the river, never."

"When," writes Mr. Coleridge, "the water of the Torridon is blue and clear from snow melting off the hills, fishing is usually hopeless."

"I myself," says Lord Breadalbane, "never had a really good day's fishing when snow has come into the river and the river has been rising by it alone. . . . This I have noticed frequently in Loch Tay."

Touching mahseer fishing.

It is not always easy to determine from a brief account of a particular experience whether there was actually snow in the water or not. Thus, regarding mahseer, General Morton says that these fish are supposed by the natives to sicken in snow-water, and he adds that when it is present the fisherman cannot do better than pack up his rods. Colonel Deane confirms the futility of fishing for mahseer in snow-broth. On the other hand, here is an experience of Colonel Stead, which seems to indicate sport with that fish when snow was in the river. It was during the Afghan War, about Christmas time, and he was fishing in the river at Kuram, which may be given as approximately 6000 feet above sea-level.

"I was," the account runs, "fishing in the river at Kuram. The country was all under snow, and the weather bitterly cold, but I got 58 lbs. weight of mahseer in about two hours' fishing. None of them were large—the best, indeed, no more than 17 lbs., but it was capital sport. I remember wading in the river, and it felt like ice."

CHAPTER IV

OF WIND

Wind necessary for lake-fishing—Other cases in which wind is wanted—Where still weather is the best: for grayling; for roach, etc.; case of char—An upstream wind best—Views of Mr. Hodgson and Sir Samuel Montagu—I. EAST WIND: Alleged malignity of east wind—Considered the best on Loch Leven—On rivers running east and west—For sea-fishing on the west coast—For bass at Brixham—Prejudice against it—Sir Henry Pottinger's opinion—Mr. Basil Champneys on the need for a broader study of wind in fishing —Mr. Sydney Buxton's experience—East wind favourable on east coast rivers—Explanations by Mr. Hall and Mr. Earl Hodgson—Evidence favourable to east wind: on the Sand River; for Thames trout; on the Otter—Other cases—Evidence against it—Exceptional cases of unexpected success — General verdict—II. NORTH WIND: In sea-fishing; an uncommon wind —N.E. wind usually even worse than E.—Exceptions to this—Conflicting opinions—III. WEST WIND: On an east coast — Note by Sir Henry Seton-Karr— Opinions favourable to west wind—IV. SOUTH WIND: Evidence in favour of it—S.E. and E.S.E.—In praise of S.W.—Quarter unimportant so long as upstream —Sport in a "Helm" wind—A veering wind bad— The same wind not suited to all seasons.

VIEWED broadly in all its relations, wind is, so far as the fisherman is concerned,

perhaps the most important of all weather
conditions.   Of itself, it may, according to its direction upstream or down,
render fly-fishing pleasant and profitable,
or the reverse.   Its absence may, on
the still water of lakes, put fly-fishing
out of court altogether.   In sea-fishing,
it may blow off the land and thus ensure
a calm sea and immunity from the dread-
ful condition in which, as the historian
relates of Philip the Handsome, the fisherman is "unquyeted in mynde and bodie."
Even apart from its intrinsic influence on
sport, wind is viewed apprehensively on
account of the rain, hail, or snow that it
may bring on its wings, or the sudden fall
in temperature, which, to the destruction
of the natural fly, may result when it
blows from an unfavourable quarter.
Apart, then, from its direction, it must
be apparent that the mere occurrence
and force of wind may be of the greatest
importance.   As a general rule, the fly-
fisher looks for the best trout on the most
windy days and, in consequence, uses his

largest flies, but even this has its exceptions.

The one case in which some sort of wind is generally regarded as an absolutely essential condition of good fishing is that of lakes, in which, in the absence of either tidal ebb and flow or the movement of running water, the surface is too still on a windless day for any style of fishing more artistic than trailing the flies astern of a moving boat. This in a measure overcomes the difficulty by both creating an artificial ripple in the wake of the boat and presenting the lures at a greater distance from the fisherman than he could reach by casting without a wind at his back, but it is at best a makeshift in no great favour with any one who can throw a fly. As a rule, those who fish in lakes like as strong a wind as possible, so long as the boat is navigable. Colonel Deane writes that he has had some of his best sport on lakes by staying out in gales until it would have been dangerous to remain on the water any longer.

Wind is considered equally necessary for spinning for pike in lakes. Mr. Barker writes that in loch-fishing for salmon or sea-trout in the Hebrides, a moderately strong wind is also desirable.

Writing of wind generally, and of wind from the S.W. in particular, Mr. Shering-ham expresses a preference for plenty of it, with waves on the water, for pike, and a good deal for salmon. For trout in a lake, he likes enough to produce a ripple and no more, and he likes a fair share when float-fishing for chub. Even on many rivers, wind of some kind is a condition of success. On the Towy, for instance, the worst possible day for the fisherman is one with clouds and no wind. *Other cases in which wind is wanted.*

There are, on the other hand, many fish and styles of fishing for which a perfectly still day, without a breath stirring, is generally admitted to be most favourable to sport. Thus, Mr. Sheringham, while liking wind for chub when float-fishing, prefers an absolutely still day, with a very hot sun, when catching the *Where still weather is the best :*

same fish on the fly. He is also an advocate of quite still weather for any fly-fishing in mountain streams, as well as for roach, bream, carp, tench, perch for grayling; and grayling. As regards the last, Mr. Rolt shares this preference. "Unsettled weather," he writes with reference to grayling fishing, "is inimical to their taking well. . . . With half a gale blowing, the grayling-fisher's bag will be empty. Three days recently spent on the Itchen will exemplify this. On the first day, the glass was steady. There was not a breath of wind, and the result of fishing from 9 till 5 was nine brace of grand fish. Days two and three were very windy, so much so that casting was impossible in the best stretches of the river open to the angler. The catch for the two days came to only 4½ brace of medium-sized fish. Again, on the Wylye one day, there was a perfect hurricane of wind and rain, and at the close of a long fight with the elements the bag showed two brace of fish just over the limit size of 11 inches. In the night the wind moderated somewhat, and, by trying sheltered spots next day, five brace of magnificent grayling were secured, the largest weighing 2 lbs. 2 oz."

This preference for calm weather in fishing is confirmed by Mr. Sydney Buxton. "Exactly contrary to wet-fly fishing," he writes, "any wind is to my mind a drawback and a nuisance in dry-fly fishing; and a heavy, boisterous wind both alarms the fish and blows the fly off the water, and so in both respects tends to spoil the rise."

When fishing in strong gales for roach, for roach, etc Mr. Rolt suggests a choice of quiet spots, for, he says, roach will not take a bait which, in sympathy with the float, travels down the swim in unnatural fashion. "Gudgeon," says Lord Desborough, "are perhaps the only Thames fish for which windy weather cannot be regarded as good."

Wind may moreover suit a particular case of char. fish in one locality, yet not in another.

Thus, Mr. Bryden has taken char freely in Loch Tay as soon as a breeze sprang up suddenly on a hot August day. On the other hand, Admiral Kennedy writes that the char in his lake in Sweden rise freely all over the water on calm, hot mornings, but are put down the moment a breeze ruffles the surface. Colonel Davies-Cooke cites a similar case of trout refusing to rise in a ripple in the Bann River, the only water in his experience in which this is the case. The professional fishermen of the locality confirm this result of his observations.[1]

An upstream wind best.

The temperature of the wind is more important than the quarter from which it blows, but the most essential condition of all for the fisherman's comfort and success is that it shall blow upstream. An upstream wind, it is to be observed, not merely favours upstream casting, but

[1] It may be noted that fly-fishing for billet (coal-fish) on Filey Brigg is possible only in an offshore (W.) wind and absolutely calm water. With any curl on the waves, local anglers fish with bait for codling only. Lord Desborough also tells me that all his best sport with tarpon was on the calmest days, with clear water.—F. G. A.

also, by blowing in a direction contrary to the run of the water, makes a better ripple.

"Excepting in the dusk and at night," Views of Mr. Hodgson and Sir Samuel Montagu. writes Mr. Earl Hodgson, "wind is desirable on lakes and on the flat parts of streams.   Otherwise, it is not in itself, I think, a cause of either good or bad sport.   It is only a symptom of the cause, or of some of the causes.   For example, a wind such as that which often comes before thunder is no use at all, and, as has been indicated, the absence of wind at nightfall, and until the dawn, is not a disadvantage."

Sir Samuel Montagu, writing with reference to his fishery on the Itchen, confirms the absence of significance of wind *per se*.   Unless accompanied by hail or heavy rain, he says that it has no appreciable effect on sea-trout fishing in that water.

It is, in fact, manifestly impossible to lay down any law as to the best or worst wind for any particular fish or mode of fishing without reference to the position of the lake or river, or even for any water without regard to the season, for, as will presently be shown, different winds suit different waters, or even the same water at different seasons of the year. Thus, drawing on a long and wide experience, Sir Thomas Esmonde is of opinion that he has killed trout in practically every wind.

It remains to consider the winds in order. Precedence is given to that from the east, as, besides being of great importance in fishing, it has been more unscientifically criticised than any other.

I. East Wind

Alleged malignity of east wind.

"There is," writes Chetham, in the *Angler's Vade-Mecum*, 1689, "a secret malignity in the east wind that generally abates fishes' appetites and desire of baits."

Considered the best on Loch Leven, etc.

Is there? Those who fish Loch Leven, or the Tweed, Bandon, or most rivers on the east side of Britain, where, coming off the sea, it blows milder than on the west, or in salt water on the west side, where it gives calm seas, or for bass off Brixham, where it imparts a desirable curl to the waves of Torbay, would pooh-pooh Master Chetham's alleged malignity and make him a present of the wind from any other quarter.

It was unreservedly condemned by many of the older angling writers, but it must be borne in mind that their standpoint was in most cases limited by a very narrow horizon, since many of them knew only the south-country streams.

There are, no doubt, localities in which an east wind puts fish off the feed. Prejudice against it. Nevertheless, much of the prejudice which exists against it is a matter of tradition rather than of actual experience. This attitude on the part of fishermen may in part be accounted for by the depressing influence which this wind has on many people, notably on those subject to neuralgia, whom I have known to suffer acutely during its prevalence in places as far apart as Melbourne and Gibraltar. So good a sportsman as Sir

Henry Pottinger, while bound to admit extenuating circumstances, gives it no quarter. " Is there," he asks, " a fly-fisher for either salmon or trout who does not hate the east wind ? In trout fishing it may, I think, be regarded as almost fatal to sport, that is to say, the genuine bitter E. or N.E. wind so characteristic of an English spring, accompanied by black and gloomy skies. There is a mitigated form of east wind in summer, nearly soft, and far less deadly an enemy. Salmon are less affected by it, I think, than trout. In Norway, at all events, I have had good sport with a cold E. wind blowing all the time I was fishing. In pike fishing, the bitter N.E. wind is said, probably with truth, to help any angler bold enough to face it, as witness Kingsley's fine lines :—

> ' . . . hunger into madness
> Every plunging pike.' "

Reference was made above to the

manner in which, for want of broader
experience, seventeenth-century angling
writers vituperated the east wind, and
Mr. Basil Champneys summarises these
limitations at some length :—

"Certain general rules have been laid
down, which apply, though with more or
less frequent exceptions, to one method
of angling and have been taken to cover
all other kinds, to which they are altogether inapplicable. Some of these, no
doubt, are survivals from an earlier
period, when the only mode of fishing in
general use was bottom-fishing. On this
most of the maxims of Izaak Walton will
be found to be based. Such rules as that
a south or west wind is favourable, a
north or east wind unfavourable, to sport
would be applicable mainly to this old-
fashioned method, whereas, in the more
complex and various methods of fishing
now in vogue, many other considerations
would have to be taken into account, and
the whole subject should now be studied
from a more scientific and comprehensive

Mr. Basil
Champneys
on the need
for a
broader
study of winc
in fishing.

point of view, when it will be found that
the effect of weather upon sport will vary
not merely with the kind of fish, but with
the nature of its chief food, with the state
of the water, the direction of the current,
and other conditions too numerous to
specify."

Writing generally as to the best
wind for dry-fly fishing, Mr. Champneys
continues :—

"To secure the natural appearance of
the fly against a strong downstream wind
is almost an impossibility, and the dry-
fly fisherman will probably prefer to take
his chance of an upstream breeze from
the quarters generally considered unfavourable, viz. north or east, rather than
of a downstream wind from a quarter
usually held to be more conducive to
sport. But for dry-fly or wet, this
ordinary division between favourable and
unfavourable quarters requires some
degree of revision. It is not, in fact,
so much a question of the quarter from
which the wind happens to be blowing at

a particular time or spot, as of the quality
of the wind affecting the temperature of
the water. Now, in the first place, the
effect will not be immediate. A change
from a warm to a cold quarter must take
some time to produce a change in the
fly-hatching condition of the water; also
a wind actually coming from the east in
some particular locality may be but a
partial or subsidiary current and may
possess the quality of that from another
quarter, say the south. These considerations may account for the frequency of
the exceptions, which are more than
sufficient to 'prove the rule.' In fact,
in order fully to analyse the applicability
of the general law, it would be necessary
to ascertain in each instance what wind
had previously prevailed when the
change took place, and whether the
present breeze was a true wind of a
quality determined by passage over
remote regions, or a mere back eddy."

Mr. Champneys' lucid and suggestive
statement of the case might well serve as

an introduction to the whole subject of fishermen's weather.

The opinion of a very experienced dry-fly fisherman is of interest in this place, by way of showing that even the much-blamed east wind may bring luck in its train. Mr. Sydney Buxton, having admitted that he prefers a S.W. to an E. wind, adds: "However, an incident on the Itchen, late in last season (1905), has rather shaken my theory and belief. Arriving one evening, in the middle of August (16th), I found raging a 'beasterly easterly' wind. I execrated my luck, for only once that season had I enjoyed a S.W. wind, and it did seem hard that in August I should still be pursued by a downstream wind. The following day was very bright, and, sure enough, the east wind was still there, though fortunately not heavy. But something possessed the trout, perhaps the August E. wind braced them up.[1]

[1] Mr. Russell writes that, although E. wind is considered bad on the west side of Scotland, he has caught trout freely

"Anyhow, I made what would have been a big bag on this reach during the cream of the season, and what for August was remarkable, *i.e.* 15 fish weighing 21 lbs,. besides putting back six and being broken by four. That this success was almost entirely, if not wholly, due to luck and not to skill was shown by the result of the following day's fishing. The east wind had by then changed to a blustering and rather cold south-west wind, and, though I lost several fish, I killed only two (in the morning) and neither of them large. Further, the fish on the first day took boldly and were all well hooked; indeed, I did not lose one, except those that broke me. But on the second day they rose gingerly, and either failed to hook at all, or were so lightly hooked that most of them soon came unfastened. I do not and cannot attempt to account for the extraordinary

in that district during an evening E. wind after a hot mid-summer's day. Here also, perhaps, as in Mr. Buxton's experience, is the result of a bracing breeze after a day of enervating heat.

disparity of the two days—a disparity which would not so much have surprised me if the result had been reversed.

"On another day, earlier in the year, on the Beane, with the Mayfly up, though rather over, I found on arrival a heavy N.E. wind, with rain, and, though I prowled about for some considerable time, I saw not a single fly nor a rising fish, and gave it up as hopeless."

East wind favourable on east coast rivers.

It has been noted that on Loch Leven and the Tweed an east wind is favourable to sport. The late Canon Beechey told me that when he fished the latter river somewhat regularly every spring during the seventies, east wind was considered the very best. Wherever it is an upstream wind (*i.e.* on rivers flowing eastward) the same rule obtains with very few exceptions, of which, however, the Aberdeenshire Dee must be regarded as one (R. T. C.). Such rivers are the Haddingtonshire Tyne, on which it is excellent (R. N.), and the Bandon, of which Mr. Conner writes : " Apart from

the condition of the water, the great
essential is wind. The river runs from
west to east, and I find either wind
equally good for fishing, but I notice
that the salmon throw themselves much
more freely in a westerly (downstream)
wind than in an easterly."

It is the fact of its blowing upstream
on these east coast rivers which makes
it such a favourite with those who fish
on that side. "The wind itself, as usual
near the coast," writes Mr. Hall, "is apt
to be somewhat boisterous, half a gale
from the north-west, or a stiff breeze,
with a cloudless sky, being conditions
absolutely opposed to sport. A light
north-east wind, drawing inland with the
tide and moderating the heat of a July
sun,[1] is here the most favourable condition of the weather that can be experienced. Curiously enough, the prevailing west winds, blowing upstream in
similar streams on the west coast, are a
grievous inconvenience to anglers on the

[1] Cf. Mr. Buxton and Mr. Russell *supra*.

east side, who have to fish downstream with a salmon-rod. Finally, it may be observed that, in the East Anglian fishery referred to, it is possible at all times to fish nearly half its available length against the wind, which eddies remarkably in the valley crowned with woods. The fish, however, do not seem to rise in this false current with much spirit, even when it does not make the water too rough for dry-fly work." Mr. Earl Hodgson offers the following intelligible explanation why the east wind should be less prejudicial to sport on the east side: "Trout in waters near the east coast are not always, as those in the midlands and west often are, put down by the east wind. This I attribute to the fact that in daytime throughout the season the wind is usually from the sea, land conducting heat more readily than water; and that thus, near the east coast, an east wind in daytime is a normal condition, to which the fish are adapted." This recalls Colonel Bairnsfather's "normal weather" theory.

Although, as will presently be shown, an east wind is regarded as fatal to sport on a number of rivers, many correspondents are by no means unfriendly to it. The following are some of the favourable opinions :—

"As regards trout taking in east wind; Evidence while wind from this quarter is generally favourable to east wind: unfavourable, especially for lake-fishing, there are curious exceptions. Loch Leven notably fishes best in a steady east breeze, and on rivers trout will often rise, especially in strongly ruffled pools, when the river is from the opposite direction, or even from the north." (A. M. S.)

"A gentle E. wind has rarely interfered with salmon fishing on days when fish seemed to be in the humour to rise; and I have known the wind veer from N. to E. without putting them off the rise." (R. B.)

"A much-libelled wind. In many on the Sand places, such as Lochs Ard and Leven, it River; is the very best. Whenever it is an upstream wind, it is likely to be the best for salmon and trout. In the Sand River (S. Norway), the E. wind, being downstream, makes salmon run fast and rise badly." (G. A. D.)

for Thames trout ;

Mr. Wheeley has caught Thames trout in weirs in bitterly cold E. wind and bright sun, a success for which he gives a curious explanation. The cold wind, he thinks, puts down the bleak in the river, which makes the one used for bait irresistible in the resulting famine.

on the Otter.

"An E. wind is at times good on the river Otter, particularly early in the season, but a high red sand cliff on the left bank of that river shelters the water from its keenness, which may have something to do with the result." (J. E. S.)

Other cases.

"E. wind and a fall of temperature in Merionethshire often increase the desire of both salmon and sewin to take a bait, whether fly or minnow." (C. E. M. E.)

"All my best days on trout waters have been distinguished by sunshine and east wind." (G. T. B.)

"Trout and sea-trout may be caught in E. wind in the Tully and Goola lakes, Connemara." (G. F.)

"There is a large mountain tarn in Carmarthenshire, on which trout rise only in an E. wind, possibly because that alone gives a suitable ripple." (W. W. F.)

"One of the best winds (N.E. is the other) for reservoir-fishing for rainbow-trout in April and May." (H. C. G.)

There is, however, no difficulty in mustering similar evidence against the wind from this quarter. The following are examples of this :— Evidence against it.

"On the Dee here (Corwen) was a remarkable hatch of fly — pale watery duns, methought — but with a pestilent E. wind, and not a fish moving, except samlets, though there are both grayling and trout in the river." (H. T. S.)

"Bad for Tay salmon." (W. O. D.)

"Fatal for trout in the Cloonaghmore River, Mayo." (G. F.)

"I used to feel satisfied, in fishing for spring-salmon in Scotland, that with an

E. wind and bright sun it was as well to put up one's rod." (C. E. D.)

"On an experience of fishing in Norway and Lapland covering seventeen years, I should regard E. wind as fatal to a rise of brown trout in those countries." (H. B. B.)

"The worst day in Donegal is when a harsh E. wind is blowing with either a dull leaden sky or a bright sun." (W. E.-J.)

"Bad for carp and tench." (C. H. W.)

"E.N.E. is one of the worst winds for the Fowey River." (C. B. R.)

"E. wind often puts pollack a little off the feed and conger still more so." (C. O. M.)

"E. wind early in the season means dry, cold weather and usually frost. If it lasts long, the water will become so cold that trout will go off their feed and revert to winter conditions." (J. W. E.)

Several correspondents, unwilling or unable to commit themselves to definite praise or condemnation of E. wind, are content to admit its frequent interference with sport and to chronicle cases of exceptional success which they have had in it. Among these are the following :—

"In May 1891 I started one day with my brother to fish the lower end of my water. The Slaney was low and very clear, and the day about the very worst I ever saw for fishing, with a steel-blue sky, blazing sun, and cold, boisterous E. wind. We got down to the bottom pool, a long, dead stretch of water, full of fish and well ruffled with the wind ; but, thinking it a hopeless day, we sat on the bank for some time in a most despondent mood. At last I determined to fish the pool, no easy task, as the wind was blowing dead across in my face. About my third cast I rose a fish, and, after a rest, cast over him again, got hold of him, and killed him. My brother then started fishing, and in three hours we killed six fish in about half a mile of water, and we must have risen about twenty. A more hope-

Exceptional cases of unexpected success.

less looking day it would be difficult to imagine." (R. St. L. M.)

Lord Suffolk informs me that Mr. Barker, who owns the Fairford water on the Coln, has seen an occasional trout taken in bitter E. wind.

" I have had good sport with an easterly wind, but, I think, always with a steady or rising glass. I have been in rivers where, evening after evening, at sundown a N.E. wind has put nearly every fish down, but I look on squally weather, from whatever quarter, as the angler's *bête noire*." (B. G. D.-C.)

" I once caught a salmon in the loch above the river (Torridon) when the wind was E., but as a rule I find even sea-trout shy in such a case." (G. C.)

" Once in a strong E. gale, with heavy rain, I caught nine salmon in the Deveron and rose many more. The fish ceased to rise as the water became thick." (The late Lady Bridge.)

" As regards the loch-trout in Orkney, E. wind is very puzzling. As a rule it is not good, but I have had some of my best days with E. wind and a cloudless sky." (A. M. S. G.)

On the whole perhaps, excepting for such lochs as lie E. and W., for rivers debouching on the east coast, on which it is the upstream wind, the verdict is against east wind. It is associated in the angler's maledictions with that from the north. General Dalton regards them as equally bad for salmon. Mr. Rolt associates them with the worst conditions for grayling. They accept, in fact, the old rhyme, which runs —: General verdict.

> South winds and west
> For fishin' are best.
> North-east and east
> No good in the least.

II. NORTH WIND

The north wind is not so often on its trial, and there is some lack of evidence. Its chief significance is along the south coast, where it is the joy of the salt-water angler, since for him it means calm seas. In sea-fishing ;

As a matter of fact, his satisfaction is tempered with other feelings, for better sport is as a rule enjoyed with ground-fish during a gentle breeze from the south-west, as in it the fish feed better and also congregate more on the inshore rocks and other grounds, whereas a strong off-shore breeze from the N. is very apt to drive them out into the deeper water.

an uncommon wind. When we come to think of it, a N. wind, pure and unalloyed by a touch of E. or W., is about the least common of all. The intervening winds, such as N.E. and N.W., are more usual, and they will be considered in this place, as their influence on fishing is in great measure due to the element of N.

N.E. wind usually even worse than E As a rule, a N.E. wind is, if anything, considered worse for fishing than E. As Lord Granby puts it: "Any wind which has any amount of N. in it is the worst possible one in which to go trout fishing. The more N. it is, the worse."

"In Banffshire rivers, a northerly wind spoils both fly- and worm-fishing." (J. C.)

CASTING INTO AN AWKWARD CORNER

Yet even this has its exceptions. "In the North of England, good sport is sometimes had with trout in cold N.E. winds." (C. G. B.)

"N.E. wind is good for rainbow-trout in reservoirs in April and May, the fish taking the fly during, or immediately after, rain showers." (H. C. G.) Exceptions to this.

"On 25th April 1882 I was leaving home in the afternoon and wanted to take a fish with me. There was a cold N.E. wind on the North Esk, and I expected a blank. I made my first cast about 10.30, and by 12 had four salmon and lost another, all beautiful fish, though not large." (C. M'I.)

General O'Callaghan writes, with absolute correctness for some waters, that cold N.E. winds are often fatal to trout · fishing, because in them no fly hatches out. Mr. Buxton is, however, able to communicate the following interesting dissentient view :—

"On the other hand, I have noticed that a cold day sometimes produces the heaviest and strongest hatch of fly, and that the fish, perhaps invigorated and braced, will occasionally rise best with the N.E. wind, though the casting is thereby rendered more difficult."

Major Boulton, though regarding a due E. wind as hopeless, remembers a spell of N.E. wind in which he had one of his best days with salmon in the Outer Hebrides. On that occasion he hooked no fewer than fourteen fish in a little over three hours.

Conflicting opinions.

The wind from due north is regarded with mingled feelings. On the Exe and Otter it is always considered bad. It is bad for salmon fishing in the Tay (W. O. D.), but fair for fishing in Donegal if not too harsh (W. E.-J.), for brown trout in Norway and Lapland (H. B. B.), and for a loch near Edinburgh, which lies E. and W. (A. W. B.). For fishing in Lough Conn it is exceptionally good (J. J. D.).

To N.W. wind the only important reference in the whole of my correspondence is made by Sir Colman Rashleigh, who describes it as "one of the worst" for the Fowey River.

III. West Wind

As regards a westerly wind, opinions On an east are unanimous, excepting in the case of coast; those east-coast rivers on which, as pointed out on an earlier page by Mr. Hall, it blows downstream, and is consequently a nuisance to the fly-fisher. In sea-fishing on the east coast, however, as well as on such portions of the coast of Devon as face the east, a west wind gives calm water, but it is also apt to bring rain. The quarter of the world in which I remember appreciating it most as the harbinger of smooth seas was on the east coast of New South Wales, between Botany Bay and the mouth of the Hawkesbury River. In that region it was impossible to go out after schnapper and other ocean-fish in boats with any enjoyment, unless the wind blew off-shore from the west, which was, however, its prevalent quarter during the winter months.

Note by Sir Henry Seton-Karr.

How essential to sport a W. wind may be for some rivers is evident from a note sent by Sir Henry Seton-Karr on a certain pool, which he knows well, below Ballyshannon Bridge, on the Irish Erne . . . "which is worth a long day's journey to fish, provided only the weather conditions are favourable. It is always well stocked with salmon from June to the end of September, when the rod-fishing closes, but it is only worth—and well worth—fishing in a strong westerly breeze, even a gale, when there is a wave a foot high on the pool. It is, under these conditions, hard work getting out the line, but the salmon then take the fly, dashing through the wave with a freedom that they show under no other circumstances. I can only infer that this particular state of the water imparts some peculiar attraction to the appearance of the fly, which the salmon find it difficult to resist."

From much evidence generally favour- able to W. wind, the following notes are selected as being of practical application in the case of specified waters :—

"Good for the Creedy, much of which, it being a spring river, is too low for angling after midsummer.' (J. D. F.-D.)

"Good for brown trout in Norway and Lapland." (H. B. B.)

"Good for Tay salmon." (W. O. D.)

"This and S.W. are best for Donegal." (W. E.-J.)

"I prefer a W. wind in the Aberdeenshire Dee and a tolerably uniform temperature." (R. T. C.)

"I like a W. wind (*i.e.* upstream) not too heavy to cast against for salmon on a west-coast river like the Kirkaig." (J. A. H.-B.)

Only, in fact, on east-coast rivers (where it blows downstream), or on Loch Leven and some other lochs similarly situated, is the W. wind opposed to the best interests of the fisherman. In these cases, however, it is hopeless. "With a

W. wind," writes Mr. Chambers, "it used
to be said on Loch Leven that the fisherman might as well put up his rod."

IV. SOUTH WIND

Though less uncommon than that from
the opposite quarter of the compass, a S.
wind, without admixture of either W. or
E., is not very common in this country.
In Australia, on the other hand, particularly in the summer months, it is not
uncommon, and a "Southerly Buster,"
bringing great seas rolling up to the
Sydney Heads from the South Pole,
makes an inspiring sight, no doubt, for a
marine painter, but puts all sea-fishing
plans in abeyance for days.

Evidence in
favour of it.

Although Izaak Walton's fondness for
a S. wind is in great measure explained
by his having fished only in the southern
counties, the wind is almost universally
liked by fishermen. In one case only,
that of the artificial loch near Edinburgh
(which lies E. and W.), referred to by

Mr. Black in earlier chapters, is a S. wind
against fishing. By others, however, its
praises are widely sung. It is described
as good for brown trout in Norway and
Lapland (H. B. B.), for loch trout in
Orkney (A. M. S. G.), and for Tay
salmon (W. O. D.). It is the best of
all winds for most of the streams of East
Devon, which flow from N. to S., thereby
making it the upstream wind.

It even seems to redeem the E. wind S.E. and
from its baneful condition, and Lord E.S.E.
Granby writes that a warm S.E. wind
is good, and E.S.E. possibly the best of
all winds, for trout fishing.

Many fishermen are also enthusiastic in In praise of
their praises of S.W. wind. For all S.W.
manner of sea-fishing on the S. coast it
is unquestionably, when not too strong,
the best of all winds. Mr. Sheringham
considers it as, on the whole, the best of
all winds for fishing. It is also described
as good for the Creedy (J. D. F.-D.), for
Tay salmon (W. O. D.), and for Donegal
fishing generally (W. E.-J.). For the

Fowey River, S.S.W. is best of all winds
(C. B. R.). Where, as on the Hampshire
rivers, which for the most part run N.E.
and S.W., it blows upstream, the S.W.
wind is, for reasons already explained,
preferable to any other, facilitating ease
and accuracy of casting, and also thereby
assisting the fisherman in rising and hooking the trout. Mr. Buxton remarks that
"the S.W. wind is unfortunately getting
scarcer and scarcer every year. As regards pleasure," he adds, "there is no
comparison between fishing with an upstream and downstream wind. On the
whole, too, I should say that the fish
rise better on the mild or warm day
that accompanies a S.W. wind than on
the cold and fairly raw day which goes
with the N.E. wind." It will not be
forgotten that, as quoted earlier in the
present chapter, Mr. Buxton himself
admits an exception in favour of a wind
from a cold quarter under certain conditions.

On the other hand, several correspondents repudiate particular qualities, Quarter unimportant so long as upstream. good or otherwise, in any wind, insisting that the only important condition is that it shall blow upstream. Thus : " I always prefer an upstream wind, from whatever quarter it blows." (C. E. M. E.)

" The old theory of S.W. wind being the best for fishing is rubbish. It does not matter whether the wind is N., E., S., or W., so long as it blows upstream. That is the essential point." (C. G. C.)

Miss Rotha Hollins sends me the Sport in a "Helm" wind. following interesting account of a good catch made in a " Helm " wind :—

" It is usually in the early part of the season that things are reversed, and now and then one has really good sport under adverse weather conditions. In March or the beginning of April, owing to the scarcity of food, the fish cannot afford to be so particular as later on in the year when there is a plentiful supply of fly on the water for them to pick and choose from.

" I remember one such day, the be-

ginning of April (1905). I was trout
fishing on the Eden between the villages
of Armathwaite and Lazonby, and had
started out about 10.30, with very little
hope of any sport. It was a cold, dull
day with a strong 'Helm' wind blowing straight downstream.

"The helm wind is well known in the
Lake district and the Eden valley as a
spoiler of all sport. It derives its name
from the helm or helmet of clouds which
forms on the fells of the Pennines and
causes the wind to circulate through the
surrounding country. Woe betide the
fisherman who has gone up for a few
days only, if he is greeted by a blast of
the helm wind on his arrival. At the
best, it means a hard battle for every fish
caught during the next few days.

"I waited awhile on the bank, but could
not see a fish moving in the pools, and it
was too early in the season for them to
have got up into the rough water, so I
knew that my only chance lay in the
tails of the streams. As soon as I com-

menced fishing, I realised that the weather
conditions were even worse than I had
anticipated. One had to wait for a lull
in the wind before attempting to cast upstream. However, things looked a good
deal brighter when, after my third or
fourth cast, I hooked and landed a fairly
nice fish. This was followed almost
directly by a second, and from the
whole-hearted way they came at the fly
(the invaluable March Brown) it was
evident that they were on the feed. I
wandered up the river, fishing every
likely bit of water, making good use
of the occasional sheltered parts, and
now and then catching an odd one or
two, but I hardly saw a rise except for
a quarter of an hour or so, about 1.30,
when they rose freely. Owing to the
difficulty in casting, it was impossible to
make the most of the short opportunity
offered, and thus I did not add as many
to my basket as I ought otherwise to
have done. After that I did very little
good, but struggled on against the wind

until about 2.30, when I determined to
stop, as it seemed useless going on longer,
and the pangs of hunger warned me that
I had brought no sandwiches with me,
and that I had a good $2\frac{1}{2}$ mile walk
home before me.

"I was surprised on emptying my bag
to find that I had twenty-two, of an
average size for the Eden. The river is
too large and swift for them ever to run
to any size, except a few old ones who
live in the pools and ignore all attempts
to catch them; but if you fish with a
10-foot rod, and hook a $\frac{3}{4}$ pounder in the
quick-running water or at the top of a
stream, he will give you all the sport you
could wish for.

"Although I had been deprived of the
angler's chief pleasure in fishing, marking
down each fish, stalking him and watching
him come up and take the fly as it floats
gently over him, I felt that fortune had
smiled on me, and that it would be a long
time before I should have another such day
under equally adverse weather conditions."

In taking leave of the subject of wind as an influence in fishing, it is desirable to draw attention to two important points. The first is, that a wind which veers all round the compass, bringing with it changeable and unsettled weather, is almost certain to spoil the angler's chances of sport, and it is even worse than if it blew steadily from an unfavourable quarter.

The other point worth considering is, that a wind from any particular quarter, which is favourable to sport in the spring season, may be just the reverse in autumn. The resulting temperature may be regarded as responsible for the difference. Mr. Buxton's instance of a bitter east wind bracing trout and making them hungry in the sultry weather of August is a case in point. Mr. Lloyd Morgan communicates another interesting illustration of the same truth. "A south-west wind," he says, "is the only one for the spring fishing in the Towy, and at that season of the year an east wind is simply fatal to sport. In summer, on the other hand, the same river yields at times very fair sport in a strong east wind." Lord Suffolk writes that east wind (in dead water) is the best for the spring fishing in the Don, whereas the same wind in autumn, with or without snow-water or frost, is the worst, and a north-west wind, with discoloured water, best.

These considerations only bear out what Mr. Champneys urged earlier in favour of a more scientific study of the very complex manner in which the force and direction of the wind may affect the angler's sport.

CHAPTER V

OF THUNDER AND LIGHTNING

Danger of lightning—Depressing effect of thunder in
the air—Weather-lore in men and fishes—Storms
follow waterways.
I. SALMON AND SEA-TROUT—Salmon rise during the storm:
in the Torridon; in the Slaney; in the North Tyne
and Irish Erne; in the Spey; in the Blackwater; in
Canada; with thunder threatening; in the Bandon
River—Evidence against thunder—Thunder good for
eel fishing.
II. BROWN TROUT—Mr. Earl Hodgson's view—Mr. Sydney
Buxton's experience—Other opinions—Sport in the
Wansbeck; in the Add—A Mayfly trout in a storm—
Colonel Davies-Cooke's luck—In the Blackwater and
Blackadder—Sir George Brown's experience—Light-
ning in the Black Forest; in the Belgian Ardennes;
in Norway—The Thames trout—Mr. Rolt on grayling
and roach—Sir Henry Pottinger's view.

THERE is, as might be expected, some Danger of lightning. little difficulty in obtaining great variety of information touching the effects of thunderstorms on sport, owing to the marked preference which most fishermen have for keeping away from the waterside under such conditions of the atmosphere. That, in short, which one correspondent refers to as "the alarm that it causes to hypersensitive men and women" tends to keep folk away from exposure on the water or beneath the trees that often fringe the bank. However conducive other extremes of the British climate may be to discomfort, or even to ill-health, lightning is the only condition which often entails bodily danger. As a further difficulty, thunderstorms are so uncommon in some districts, like Orkney (A. M. S. G.), during the fishing season that local sportsmen have no opportunity of learning their effect from experience.

Depressing effect of thunder in the air.

With all conditions of weather, scientifically considered in relation to the present inquiry, it is necessary to draw a distinction between those which merely threaten and those which are accomplished fact. Even on ourselves, "thunder in the air" has an effect of depression that can be likened only to that caused by east

wind, and all nature puts on a mood of
tension at the coming of a thunderstorm,
throwing it off the moment the storm
bursts. The passing of the thunder-
clouds seem, particularly if they break
in heavy rain, to leave the air clearer and
the world refreshed.

Since human weather-lore is very crude, Weather-lore
reason being bestowed, so far as we can n men and i
judge, at the cost of instinct, we cannot ishes.   1
always tell whether an impending thunder-
storm will burst over our heads or keep
its fury for some other spot. We watch
the familiar grey clouds working up
against the wind, but the exact locality
in which the storm will reach the break-
ing-point is matter of conjecture. As a
rule, the beasts and birds have keener
perception of such developments than
ourselves, and even trout are in many
districts put down by lightning and still
more so by the brewing of the storm.
Mr. Hall's interesting account of Norfolk
trout, unable to discriminate between
actual storms threatening the locality

and those "tempests," so called, which pass out to sea, was cited in the Introduction, and needs no further notice. Mr. Champneys points out that the prophetic instinct, which so often enables fresh-water fishes to foretell the coming of a thunderstorm, looks like a survival from a marine habitat, where alone such prescience would be needed to enable them to take shelter from the violence of the waves. No such danger threatens them in rivers, yet they appear to have retained the protective instinct, even where it is to some extent supererogatory.

Storms follow waterways.

The influence which thunderstorms may have on fishing gains added interest from the well-established fact that these phenomena follow canals and other waterways. From observations made on the Kaiser Wilhelm Canal by German officials connected with the Meteorological Survey, this tendency seems entitled to general recognition.

I. Salmon and Sea-Trout

With few exceptions, those who have given evidence on the relations between thunder and fishing are agreed that the menace of the storm rather than the storm itself is the deterrent.

"Thunder," writes Sir John Edwards-Moss, "seems to keep fish down till the storm fairly breaks; then they will often rise. . . . I have caught a salmon and played him while I could see it lightning and hear it thundering over a hill some three miles away." Salmon rise during the storm:

Mr. Gilbert Coleridge contributes an experience in some ways similar.

"It is," he writes, "a common opinion that fish will not take a fly when thunder is in the air, but I once experienced a notable exception to this rule. I had just begun to fish a pool in the Torridon when two or three brilliant flashes of lightning began to play about the top of the hills in full view of the pool, accompanied by loud peals of thunder and in the Torridon;

14

heavy rain. I was beginning to fear lest my rod should attract the lightning, and was going to leave off and take shelter, when a salmon rose and took my fly. Then, perhaps rashly, I decided to take my risk of being struck, and I soon landed my fish. I have never, before or since, heard of fish taking in like circumstances, for the flashes were most brilliant, and the thunder very loud, coming from steep precipices that almost overhang the pool."

Colonel St. Leger Moore had, while fishing the Slaney, an experience, if anything, still more remarkable of catching salmon in a storm.

in the
Slaney ;

"In April 1886," he writes, "I was fishing the river Slaney, of which I rent a considerable stretch, in apparently perfect fishing weather, the river itself being in good order and colour. I had only risen one fish up to 1.30 P.M., when black clouds came over the sky and enormous spots of rain began to fall, and a baddish thunderstorm broke. I was reeling in my line, intending to get under a rock, when I saw a fish turn under my fly. I cast again, rose, hooked and eventually landed him. I then went on down the pool, and at the tail of it I killed another fish after a good fight. In the stream below, I hooked and lost a third fish. All this time the thunder was crashing overhead. The storm ceased just after, and I did not get another fish till quite late in the evening. I had always previously thought that it was utterly useless fishing in a thunderstorm."

Other experiences of salmon caught in thunderstorms are communicated by Sir Ford North and Mr. Bagot, the latter remembering one of the best afternoons of salmon fishing in the North Tyne that he ever enjoyed, during a heavy thunderstorm near the end of September. Sir Ford North's memories of success under such conditions include days on the Irish Erne and Spey. "One day," he writes with reference to the former river, "a violent thunderstorm came up, with extreme darkness; and while the thunder

in the North Tyne and Irish Erne;

was pealing very loudly overhead, but without rain, I hooked and landed two fine salmon. So far as I could judge, I might have continued fishing with equal success, but that the rain suddenly came down in torrents, and from that time not in the Spey; a fish would stir. I had," he adds, "a similar experience on the Spey, except that on that occasion the rain came down in torrents while I was landing my first fish." This distinction between wet and dry storms is of still more importance in the case of trout, which, being more concerned than salmon with the food-supplies, are supposed to be affected by coming storms owing to their anticipation of rain and fresh stores of worms.

in the Blackwater; The foregoing cases of salmon caught during the raging of the storm were in accord with what has already been said of the fish rising under such conditions. Much more common is success immediately after the storm is over. "I have," writes Colonel Deane, "found thunder affect fishing everywhere, and when it is over the fishing is often better than it was before the storm. This I recently found to be the case in the Blackwater, where, directly after a thunderstorm, I killed three good salmon. I have found much the same to be the case in India."

More unusual is it to catch fish in that state of impending storm of which gillies in some districts speak as "fire in the air." Even with the atmosphere in this electrical condition, however, my correspondence contains cases of sport. The following are cases in point:—

"My general experience of spring in Canada; salmon in Scotland," wrote the late Sir Clinton Dawkins, "was that no fish would take in thundery weather. But I am bound to say that the last time I killed a salmon (in the Ristagouche, Eastern Canada) I found the fish rising freely in close, thundery weather. I do not know whether this is peculiar to Canada."

"I caught a salmon this year (1905) on a 'Wilkinson' fly just before a thunderstorm, but I fancy that this is very exceptional." (W.)

"Last year (1904) I caught a salmon in Little Loch Awe (above Inchnadamph) on a heavy, thundery day, about half an hour after a distant peal of thunder, which did not, however, clear the air much. It was a rather cold August day, as well as heavy and thundery." (F. C. B.)

Mr. Conner holds views on the subject opposed to the theories of which we have taken account, for he remarks that he never in all his experience knew of a salmon being taken in the Bandon River during a thunderstorm, whereas "this year, the morning before thunder commenced, fish were taking, and the day after they took well."

The foregoing successes may, however, be regarded as exceptions to the rule. The majority of salmon-fishermen condemn thunder without reservation. Sir James Fergusson "never saw any good done in it"; and Sir W. Dalgleish specifies that it spoils sport in the Tay.

LOCH TROOL

According to Sir Samuel Montagu, it is equally prejudicial to sea-trout fishing in the Itchen, and Mr. Munro Edwards, writing of Welsh streams and lakes, has found that it makes both salmon and sewin dour, though both may be caught after the passing of the storm, a view confirmed by General Dalton and some others. Perhaps the most scathing criticism of all is Mr. Barker's assurance that he regards it as "fatal, except for eels." What connection there may be between thunder and eels I do not know, but Mr. Wheeley affirms that such weather actually favours sport, if sport it can be called, with that fish. The fact is given only for the naturalist, for that any sportsman could deliberately seek to learn the best weather for catching eels is exceedingly improbable.

Thunder good for eel fishing.

II. Brown Trout

Thundery weather is regarded as hostile to trout fishing in many widely separated districts,[1] but there is also varied evidence of baskets of trout being made in spite of it.

With the helpful side of thunder in trout fishing Mr. Earl Hodgson deals from that non-committal "symptomatic" standpoint of his, which evokes the same admiration as the logic of an astute leader of modern politics.[2] "Thunder," he writes, "is a great help. That is to say, the changes of atmosphere of which thunder is a symptom are beneficent. Sometimes the trout, which have been lying low for many hours during the gradual degeneration of the atmosphere, rise well soon after the storm has broken.

---

[1] *E.g.* on the Exe and Otter (J. E. S.), in Shetland (J. S. T.), and in Banffshire (J. C.).

[2] Mr. Earl Hodgson remarks, with reference to this criticism : "My half-sheet of notepaper seems as unfortunate as Mr. Balfour's. Where is the difficulty? Take this case. Thunder is noise caused by explosions in the clouds. Is it the noise which keeps the trout down for a time before the storm? Clearly it cannot be, for there is no noise. Is it noise during the storm, or remembrance of it soon after, that brings them up again? No ; the effect results from some atmospheric change due to the lightning. Therefore thunder in its relation to the moods of trout is casual rather than causal, incidental, a mere symptom."

Almost always, if the storm has been thorough and accompanied by much rain, they give good sport for a considerable time after the storm has passed."

Mr. Sydney Buxton's view is that a thunderstorm clears the air and cheers up the trout. In illustration of its beneficial effect on chalk-stream fishing, he quotes the following :—

Mr. Sydney Buxton's experience.

"One day, a year or two ago, quite early in September, fishing in the Itchen in a N.E. wind, there had been up to 5 o'clock neither rise, fly, nor fish. There came up a sudden thunderstorm, with heavy rain, lasting for about $1\frac{1}{2}$ hours. During that time I rose, hooked and lost several fish. They rose very short. Directly the storm ceased, the fish also ceased to rise absolutely. The record bag on this fishing was, I believe, made some years ago on a day of prolonged thunderstorms."

Dr. Cheadle, writing of the same method and locality, considers that trout rise better after than during the storm.

Lord Granby takes the less hopeful
view that thunder usually puts all trout
off their feed, though he has known occasions when a storm has raged and trout
have risen simultaneously. As in the
case of salmon, trout, though as a rule
slack just before a storm, will often feed
well while it is in progress. "Thunder in
the air," the late Canon Beechey wrote to
me a few weeks before his death, "is fatal
to success in fly-fishing for trout, but
when the storm breaks, the rise is often
furious." Of brown trout in Norway
and Lapland, Dr. Baker writes: "No rise
takes place while the storm is pending.
Directly the storm breaks, the rise begins
vigorously." "Before thunder," writes
Mr. Russell, "when the atmosphere is
charged with electricity, trout do not take
a fly well, but during a thunder-rain on
one occasion I had the best rise of trout
almost that I ever remember seeing."
Major Godley, on the other hand, has
found that trout "generally rise immediately before a thunderstorm," a most

interesting opinion as the result of long experience, because it is directly opposed to the general verdict on the subject.

General Desmond O'Callaghan once made a big basket in one of the worst thunderstorms he ever stayed out in.

" This was on the Wansbeck (Northum- Sport in the Wansbeck ; berland). A black sky and impending rain kept all the fish down until about mid-day, when the storm burst. Amid vivid lightning, sheets of rain and occasional sharp hailstorms, with big (and very painful) hailstones, the fish began to rise freely. On that occasion, at any rate, the electrical conditions did not hinder the fish from feeding."

Colonel Malcolm recalls what he in the Add. describes as "the most sporting, mean-to-have-it" rise of trout in all his experience, on the river Add, which empties into Loch Crinan. This was during a heavy hailstorm and between claps of thunder pealing some little distance away.

Lord Suffolk tells me that the Dowager Lady Suffolk, an enthusiast with

A Mayfly trout in a storm.

the fly-rod, once caught a fine trout in a violent thunderstorm at Charlton (near Malmesbury) on a Mayfly in June. The weather is described as "fairly crackling at the time," and it must have been anything but encouraging to a lady to stay out in.

On the whole, trout are considered more susceptible to impending thunder than salmon. On the occasion, already referred to, on which Prof. Burkitt caught a salmon in thundery weather in Little Loch Awe, the party were also fishing for trout, but caught very few.

Colonel Davies-Cooke's luck.

Colonel Davies-Cooke, who draws attention to the manner in which trout are apt to leap and rise short, with thunder threatening, relates an extraordinary lucky day during a violent storm :—

"It hailed and rained in torrents, and there was almost continuous thunder and lightning. It was in June, about the year 1886, and the Mayfly was on. I was on the water about 9.30 A.M. and started with a Mayfly and an Alder. A heavy storm had been gathering all the morning, and at first I could do nothing; but when the storm burst, the trout began to rise, three out of four taking the Mayfly, and I was kept fully employed. I therefore took off the Alder and continued with one Mayfly, as there were many weeds and stumps. It was quite a small stream, a brook that one could cover with a line as long again as the rod. . . . I was wet to the skin in no time. By about two the storm ceased, and so did I, for the rise was over, but I had caught 22 trout weighing 17½ lbs. As far as I know, it was the best bag ever made in that water, and I have fished it for over fifty years. Alas, its glory is departed, and it is no longer worth fishing, for the good little river now supplies three water companies!"

Colonel Deane's capture of three salmon in the Blackwater, directly after a thunderstorm, has been already quoted. On the Blackadder, Mr. Noble, fishing with a friend, caught his share of a basket of fifteen trout during a raging storm.

In the Black water and Blackadder.

"We found the river very low, and it was impossible to approach the bank without the fish seeing every movement. Towards evening, a very severe thunder-storm passed over our heads : you seemed to feel the warm flash of the lightning all over you, and next day's newspapers told of people, as well as cattle and horses, killed by the storm."

After the storm has exhausted itself, or moved on elsewhere, trout, as Sir Douglas Brooke points out, often rise freely.

Sir George Brown's experience.

"On several occasions," writes Sir George Brown, "when I have been over-taken by a sudden thunderstorm, and no shelter has been available, I have observed that the fish, which have previously taken little or no notice of the fly, have risen madly, but in this connection I have also observed that while I have hooked a fish at nearly every cast, I have, probably in my anxiety to land as many as possible while the storm lasted, lost a great many before I could get them within reach of the landing-net."

Two experiences of Continental streams in districts much visited by English fly-fishers, further illustrate this biting mood of trout in storms :—

"I once had a remarkable experience in the Black Forest, in a river which opens out into a wide, still, shallow pool, which, I thought, contained only white fish. One day, in one of the most terrifying storms I was ever out in, trout rose madly all over it. This was the only time I had ever seen them rise there, and, being young, I was fool enough to stay out and make a big bag of them, though to this day I cannot understand how the rod did not attract the lightning." (G. A. D.)

Lightning in the Black Forest

"Thunder is supposed to affect fish in the same way in which it depresses or alarms hypersensitive and nervous men and women. The theory is that fish know when a storm of thunder and lightning is brewing, and that they seek shelter and refuse to feed. My own experience is that, generally speaking, fish are sluggish while thunder-clouds are gathering, but exceedingly active after the first flash of lightning. Trout often rise eagerly to the fly *during* a thunder-storm, provided that it is not accompanied by heavy rain.

.n the Belgian Ardennes ;

"While fishing in the Belgian Ardennes this autumn (1905), I found the trout of a small stream in rising humour through-out a heavy, thundery day. After the first rumble of thunder, the trout rose with increased avidity. But it must be noted that only a few drops of rain fell, and that the actual storm was of short duration. I think that during pro-longed unsettled weather, when the atmosphere is charged with electricity, fish are more or less shy and off their food." (W. M. G.)

in Norway.

During his Norwegian trips, on the other hand, Mr. Bryden found trout put off the feed by thunderstorms. "During the summer of 1893," he writes, "I enjoyed some exceptionally good brown-trout fishing in various lakes and streams

in the vicinity of the Hardanger Fjord.
This lasted from the first week in June
to about the second week in July. Then
we had thunder for some days, and the
weather became unsettled. The trout
went off extraordinarily, and, after they
had come at our lures with the wonderful
greed that Norsk trout are accustomed to
display early in the season, we could, for
about ten days, do very little with them.
From the time the fine spell was broken
by thunder, in fact to the end of July,
sport was comparatively indifferent."

We have already seen how the Thames The Thames
trout may be caught in the most in- trout.
clement weather, hail and snow apparently conducing to success in pursuit of
it. Mr. Wheeley remembers taking one
of 7½ lbs. when worm-fishing for barbel in
a fearful thunderstorm. "Evening had
set in, and the fish had to be played and
landed in the light afforded by the vivid
flashes of lightning."

Colonel St. Leger Moore once got
16 large white trout, some weighing up to

$3\frac{1}{2}$ lbs., out of a loch "with lightning playing all over the water."

Mr. Rolt on grayling and roach.

This practically concludes the evidence touching thunder, though Mr. Rolt recalls fishing in a thunderstorm for grayling, without any result beyond catching several brace of trout, which were, of course, returned to the water. He adds that roach seem to decline a bait when a storm is brewing, or even when it is raging, but that they soon recover their appetites and bite ravenously as soon as it is over.

Sir Henry Pottinger condemns thunder, as he did east wind, in general terms, and the fact of so much of his fishing having been done in Norway lends special interest to his attitude in view of Mr. Bryden's Norwegian experience just quoted.

Sir Henry Pottinger's view.

"I have," he writes, "no hesitation in saying that almost invariably thunder, especially when accompanied by vivid lightning, is the fisherman's enemy. Friends have indeed told me that they have taken fish right through a thunderstorm, but I have myself always found that it puts the fish down, and that even in thundery weather, without an actual storm, it is very difficult to get rises. After the storm has completely passed away, fish will sometimes begin to take quite freely."

In most of the chapters in this book the reader will find, and, after reading the Introduction, will have been prepared to find, considerable divergence of opinion, but in no case perhaps is this conflict of evidence more striking than in respect of thunderstorms, to which some of my correspondents seem indifferent, others actively hostile, while a few have in special cases had to thank them for better sport than they ever enjoyed in the same water under more enjoyable conditions of weather.

CHAPTER VI

OF FOG AND MIST

Actual danger of fog—Mr. Champneys' distinction between dry- and wet-fly—Experience of Welsh fishermen—Mr. Earl Hodgson's view—Mr. Sheild and
others on effects of cold mist.
I. EVIDENCE AGAINST FOG AND MIST: in trout-fishing ; in
fishing for salmon or sea-trout.
II. CASES OF SUCCESS—With salmon — Experience of Sir
Ford North—Fog in sea-fishing—Grayling feed in a
fog ; also roach — Mr. Sheringham on morning and
evening mist—Discomfort of bad weather—Moral of
the book.

Actual
danger of
fog.

WITH a few interesting exceptions, chiefly
in favour of grayling and roach, correspondents agree in condemning fog,
whether brooding on the mountain-tops
or actually lying on the surface of the
water, two characteristic positions that
are not by any means always coincident.
In a few districts, of course, fog may
actually constitute a danger even graver

228

than lightning, but these are of purely local interest in cases like that alluded to in the well-known Devonshire tag :—

> In a Dartmoor fog
> Stick to your grog,
> Or yew'll fall in a bog.

Most fishermen who have studied the influence of fog on scientific lines draw an interesting and important distinction between the ways in which this condition of the atmosphere affects fishes that rise after the perfect insect and those others that feed on the larvæ or other submerged food, or, in other words, as Mr. Champneys puts it, between dry and wet fly-fishing.   It is by checking the natural hatch, the appearance of which is usually *inter alia* a matter of temperature, that a mist on the water puts trout down. Looking back on his experiences of dry-fly fishing, Mr. Champneys is unable to recall a solitary exception to failure in foggy weather, and he has invariably found the evening rise on the Test cease abruptly as soon as an almost invisible

Mr. Champneys' distinction between dry- and wet-fly.

film has formed on the surface of the water. Fishing wet, on the other hand, in which the drowned fly must resemble an aquatic larva, he has more than once succeeded in making a good bag of trout in a dense fog.

Experience of Welsh fishermen. Intelligible as this distinction unquestionably is, it is not to be denied that there are cases in which even a sunk bait is rejected of trout while fog is about. Welsh fishermen told Mr. Gallichan, who has done much fishing in the Principality, that they found it difficult, if not impossible, to make a basket of trout with worm, once the mist descended more than halfway down the slopes of the hills. This would seem to indicate that mist on the mountain-tops is powerless to affect the rise, but such is not the case elsewhere.

Mr. Earl Hodgson's view. Of the adverse influence of fog on the fisherman's catch, Mr. Earl Hodgson takes his customary "symptomatic" view. Personally, he admits having invariably failed to make the good baskets in foggy weather, of which he has both heard and read; but, even so, he feels bound to regard fog less as the actual cause of trout not feeding than as the symptom of the cause.

One view, by no means unpopular Mr. Sheild and others on effects of cold mist. with trout-fishermen, is that the baneful effects of fog are almost wholly a matter of a fall in the temperature. "Fog or mist," writes Mr. Sheild, "is fatal to trout fishing, especially when the atmosphere is cold. Every practical trout-fisherman knows how trout never rise well in lakes when the hills are shrouded in mist. And in that most enjoyable sport, night-fishing for trout in June or July, the advent of a mist on the river will stop the most furious sport as if by magic."

Major Wynn Eyton also attributes the slackness of the trout to the sudden fall in temperature, in support of which view he remarks that "even the light evening mists, that rise over the water on summer evenings, put the fish down at once, although the surface of the water may be strewn with half-drowned flies."

I. Evidence against Fog and Mist

In trout fishing;

Whatever the causes, whether the direct result of a fall in temperature or some more subtle influence that we know nothing of, fog is regarded by most trout-fishermen as detrimental to success. This is the view taken by Lord Granby, Mr. Barrington, and many others. Of Swedish trout, Admiral Kennedy writes: "If there is mist on the mountains, or rising from the water, the fish retire at once, and the sportsman may just as well do likewise." Similarly, of Norway and Lapland, Dr. Baker says: "The rise stops directly the mist reaches the water. Even when mist is on the mountains, high above the water, the rise is poor."

Colonel Davies-Cooke considers that "sport is ended when fog or mist comes creaming over the mountain-tops."

"The white mists," writes Mr. Gallichan,

"which arise from rivers during the summer after sunset, often cause a sudden cessation of an evening rise of trout."

Nor is a condition of fog any better, in the opinion of many experienced fishermen, for salmon or sea-trout. The following extracts from letters will serve to illustrate how general this opinion is :—

"Mist on the top of the high hills is almost invariably bad for sea-trout and salmon in the Western Highlands." (J. B.)

"Evening fog generally puts an end to an evening rise. Where mist is low down on the hills, salmon rarely take well." (G. A. D.) in fishing for salmon or sea-trout.

"If a sea-fog is coming on, fish will never rise and very seldom, if ever, show. I have been out on the loveliest fishing morning, when one expected great things . . . and seen nothing. This was inexplicable till the approach of a wall of sea-fog in the afternoon solved the mystery." (J. E.-M.)

"Fog is fatal to fishing for either salmon or trout, but more especially for salmon." (C. G. C.)

"It is useless to fish for salmon in the Bandon River during a fog." (H. D. C.)

"It is not usual in the Torridon to get rises when there is a mist on the hill-tops." (G. C.)

"I distrust especially low clouds clinging to the mountain sides, which probably mean fog in the south." (A. E. G.-H.)

"I never think there is much use in fishing in the Aberdeenshire Dee for salmon when there is mist on the hills." (R. T. C.)

"On the Awe, the gillies say fish will not rise when there is a mist or clouds hanging about the hills." (J. C. R.)

"Fog is bad for sea-trout fishing in the Itchen." (S. M.)

"Mist near the surface of the water keeps salmon down." (C. G. B.)

"I should regard fog as an enemy of the salmon-fisherman." (W.)

"Fog is bad for all fishing." (C. H. W.)

These are some among many opinions
adverse to fog.

II. CASES OF SUCCESS

On the other hand, my correspondence
contains several evidences of success with
trout, salmon, grayling and roach, though
in the case of the first two these are
evidently regarded by the fishermen
themselves as exceptions to the rule.

Only two praise fog in general terms,
and that only when it is lifting, or broken
by gleams of sunshine.   Captain Edg-
worth-Johnstone writes in praise of such
a condition on Donegal waters, and Mr.
Gallichan considers fog less depressing
to fish when it occurs during a frost,
with sunshine faintly visible through it.

There are not in the whole correspondence more than three or four actual records
of good baskets of trout in foggy weather.
Sir James Fergusson has "known a great
basket of trout caught in a fog, in a
loch where the trout are often very shy."

Sir Thomas Esmonde has " often killed trout in the evening, with a slight mist on the water"; and Mr. Noble remembers on one occasion filling his basket in the Haddingtonshire Tyne, fishing from 11 P.M. until daybreak, with a thick Scotch mist about.

These are meagre evidences of good sport with trout in a fog, out of over eighty letters that make some reference to that condition of weather, and it is perhaps reasonable to conclude that it militates against sport with this fish more even than with most others.

With salmon. Not that there is much evidence of salmon taking in foggy weather, but in two cases the success was so marked that lack of it may be rather due to unwillingness of fishermen to fare forth under such miserable conditions, which are, moreover, traditionally associated with bad luck, than to actual slackness of the salmon. Thus, Sir Colman Rashleigh actually remembers having made some of his best catches in the Fowey River on still, foggy days. This qualification suggests, in view of what was said in earlier chapters of the advantage of wind, rain, or hail in imparting a ripple to the surface, that the extreme stillness commonly associated with a fog may in part be responsible for the indifferent sport enjoyed by fly-fishermen under such conditions.

The most remarkable experience of successful salmon fishing in a fog is communicated by Sir Ford North, who writes as follows :—

"You know how fatal to success in fishing a mist is supposed to be. I have often found this to be so, to my cost, in a prolonged experience. One morning, early in October, about 9 A.M., I went down to fish my water on the Spey. There was a very dense mist all round, with a frosty air, though, looking upwards, the sky seemed bright, as if the mist would clear in an hour or so and leave a fine day. When my rod and line were ready, I did not dream of beginning to fish till the mist cleared

Experience o
Sir Ford
North.

away. My gillie said, however, that we ought not to waste time, but I derided the idea of fishing in such a state of the atmosphere. However, I yielded to his remonstrance, and in three-quarters of an hour, before the fog had gone, I had two salmon on the bank. Then the day became beautifully fine and bright, and I never rose another fish, though I have often caught fish on equally bright days. My gillie, a very sharp, shrewd fellow, rested his advice to begin on instinct rather than on experience. I am not myself partial to fishing in a fog. I have often found it painfully useless, and I quote this instance not as establishing any rule, but rather as furnishing an exception to one."

Fog in sea fishing.

Of fog in sea-fishing I have little experience. Such weather is so dreaded at sea that every precaution is taken to avoid it. Few ever dream of embarking with any probability of fog during the day, and fewer still stay out on the grounds after the - first faint indication

of thick weather.   One occasion I recall,
however, in the estuary of the river Teign,
where we were perfectly safe one June
morning, bass fishing just within the bar,
for the simple reason that no tug or other
vessel would dare to run in or out of that
narrow waterway until the fog lifted.
During a thick fog off the moor, which
completely enveloped banks less than fifty
yards on either side of the boat, there
was a mad rise of bass all over the water,
and I succeeded in catching a number
of small "herring-size" fish on the fly—
one of the few occasions on which I have
tried that method, as I fish as a rule for
the bigger bass, and these take only the
living sand-eel.   I can also remember
making a great catch of whiting off the
Eddystone Lighthouse while anchored
in an impenetrable fog.

The grayling appears at times to feed Grayling feed
in spite of fog.   Mr. Sheringham includes in a fog;
it with pike and perch among those fish
that are not invariably put down by foggy
weather; and Mr. Rolt remarks on the

same subject : "When the thick mists of autumn steal over the land, the theory is that fishing is no good. On several occasions this has been proved erroneous in the case of grayling. In the early morning, too, before the watery vapour has risen off the water, grayling have been caught with the sunk fly." Mr. Marston also has known grayling (and trout) rise on misty evenings in the Itchen, when at times it was impossible to see more than thirty or forty yards over the water.

ılso roach.

The roach is another fish which is even said to feed keenly during a fog. Several writers allude to this peculiarity of roach. "On the Norfolk Broads," writes Mr. Gallichan, "the 'water-smoke,' which rises suddenly, sometimes in the middle of a warm day, does not appear to affect bream and roach." Mr. Marston remembers catching roach as fast as he could land them when the fog was so thick that he could only just see his float. Mr. Rolt also notes that roach bite keenly in foggy weather, "though," as he quaintly adds, "fishing when the end of the roach-pole can scarcely be seen is hardly an exhilarating amusement." Mr. Matthews recalls an even yet more striking success with roach in a fog so dense that, while fishing, he could hear other anglers talking, but was unable to see them. It was in the river Colne, and on this occasion he left Waterloo with a number of members of the Piscatorial Society in a typical London fog, and the party caught over 100 lbs. of roach.

Writing of the effect of fog on coarse fish, Mr. Sheringham distinguishes between harmless morning mist, on the melting of which, about 5.30 A.M., the fish feed greedily, from evening mist, which he considers fatal to all non-migratory fish. The summer mist of the moorland Mr. Sheringham regards as practically a form of rain, and, as such, in no way prejudicial to trout fishing in those localities where it occurs.

Mr. Rolt's remark above, touching the

Mr. Sheringham on morning and evening mist.

16

lack of exhilaration in fishing for roach in a thick fog, brings us appropriately, at the conclusion of the book, back to the programme that bad weather would be discussed without any regard for its connection with the sportsman's discomfort. The horrors of the British climate have been contemplated in the foregoing pages from the standpoint of fishes rather than from that of men. Indifference to unspeakable weather is among the keen fisherman's pronounced eccentricities. Those, in fact, who are not prepared to bear a good deal of discomfort from this source will hardly find outdoor sport of any kind to their liking within the limits of the British Isles.

To those, however, who snap their fingers at torrid sun or pouring rain, who laugh at the sting of hailstones or the bite of frost, who reck not of the danger from lightning or from fog, this book offers one advice, and that is, that they should never despair of good sport under conditions that tradition and the text-books

" CHANGING THE FLY

condemn as hopeless. If the evidence collected in the foregoing pages means anything, it means that all manner of fish, game fish, coarse fish and sea-fish, are liable to take a fly or other lure in any and every condition of the atmosphere, in any wind, in all temperatures. To him is the victory who persists in the face of apparent hostility on the part of the elements. Yet it is hoped that, although the results of the conclusions arrived at in these pages may thus be summed in a single sentence, the records and experiences by which, step by step, these have been arrived at will not be without practical value and considerable interest for the sportsman who has a mind for the rhyme and reason of his art, and who seeks to know a little more than merely how to throw a fly and play a salmon.

APPENDIX

BEST AND WORST WEATHER (SPRING AND AUTUMN) FOR CERTAIN WATERS

Name of Water.	Season.	Best Conditions.	Worst Conditions.	Source of Information.
Bandon	Spring	Open weather, and E. or W. wind; water clearing after rise.	Frost, snow, cold wind.	H. D. Conner, Esq.
	Autumn	Very little fishing.		
Blackadder	Spring	Open weather, with E. wind in dead water.	Hard frost, with snow-water.	R. Noble, Esq.
Coquet	Spring	No salmon fishing in spring.	Stormy, unsettled weather, with water rising, or a dead low, clear water.	J. J. Hardy, Esq.
	Autumn	Good full water, black or beer colour; moderate W. wind.		
Dee	Spring and Autumn	Open weather, W. or S.W. breezes, and water steadying to normal after a flood.	Snow - water, E. wind, dead low water.	Sir H. Seton-Karr.
Don	Spring	Open weather; W. wind in strong streams, E. wind in dead water.	Hard frost, with cold winds.	The Earl of Suffolk.
	Autumn	Open weather; N.W. wind; normal, dis-coloured water.	Hard frost, snow-water, E. wind.	

				Sir Samuel Montagu.
Itchen (Hants)	Autumn	All but East wind; drizzling and dull ◼◼; water slightly coloured.	Frost and East wind; bright sunny ◼◼.	
Kent (Westmorland)	Spring and Autumn	◼◼, ◼◼ weather; S.W. and N.W. wind; water on the low side for day, and low for night-fishing.	Frost, mist, or fog; high ◼◼s, especially from N. and E.; white clouds; ◼◼.	R. Bagot, Esq.
Loch Lomond	All seasons	Blustering wind with rain; S. or S.W. wind; dull skies.	Dead ◼◼; hard, cold wind; threatening rain.	W. ◼ ◼◼, Esq.
Orchy	Spring	Open weather, and W. ◼◼d, with rainy cl uds.	Hard frost, with cold N.E. winds or snow-water.	A. Mayo Robson, Esq.
	◼◼n	Open ◼◼r, with W. wind; ◼◼d, with discoloured ◼◼r.	Hard frost, snow-water, or N. wind.	
Severn	Spring	Open weather; no ◼◼-water; S.W. winds and high rainfall.	Snow-water and hard frost.	J. W. Willis Bund, Esq.
	Autumn	S.W. winds and high rainfall.	Very dry weather.	
Slaney	Spring	W. or S.W. wind, ◼◼ard open weather.	Hard frost.	Colonel St. Leger Moore.
Stour (Christchurch) (coarse fish)		Open ◼◼r.	After ◼◼y rain.	H. Newlyn, Esq.
Tawe (Carmarthen)	Spring	Open weather; fresh W. winds or showers.	E. winds.	W. Warde Fowler, Esq.
	Autumn	Open weather, and low water.	Wet, cold weather.	

Name of Water.	Season.	Best Conditions.	Worst Conditions.	Source of Information.
Tay	Spring	Mild; W. or S.W. wind; medium-sized water, not discoloured.	N. wind, with frost and snow.	Sir W. O. Dalgleish, Bt.
	Autumn	Fine, mild; W. or S.W. wind, with cloudy sky, or intermittent sunshine.	Cold winds, and water discoloured with snow-broth.	
Teign	Spring Early Jun	Mild; S. or W. wind. Dull, with sufficient rain from a warm 1 ter.	Bight, with E. wind. Bright, dry weather.	H. Michelmore, Esq.
Thames (coarse fish)	Spring, ten, and Winter	Open weather, with S.W. wind; hik water for roach, clear for chub, perch, or pike.	Foggy weather, with mch snw in ter; E. wind; yt occasionally for Thames trout. [Fishing much spoilt by traffic.]	C. H. Wheeley, Esq.
	Summer	Dry, squally weather, dns. S.W. wind,		
Thurso River and Loch More	Spring (ery little river-fishing after 1st Apil)	Frequent spates from rain or melted snw. In Loch More, after 1st April; not too many gales; N.W. wind best for iver; wet sen.	River frozen ver, all except shallow streams, where fish do not rest. Too frequent gales dirty the water; very low ter.	F. G. Enys, Esq.
Torridon	Spring and Jun	W. or S.W. wind; luds and rain; plenty of ter.	N. or E. ind, or calm, low ter.	Hon. Gilbert Coleridge.

Tweed .	Spring	Low, lear water; W. ind.	Stormy wtr, with strong W. nds, snow-broth, and stig wtr.	J. J. Hardy, Esq.
	Autumn	Fair- mid water, blackish colour; dull sky; W. and S.W. winds.	Rising wtr full of leaves; ı nttled thr.	
Usk .	Spring	Bt hght of water for salmon fing on the Usk Upper Association Mr is from 2' 6" in to 8". Open weather. Strong wtr at 1' 6". In slow wtr wind is wanted, but if nd nits one pool it ny not suit another; ery title is nd.	Low ter with bght sun. If the are plenty of a lmn in the ı ier the salmon will not rise at the fly.	Horace S. Lyne.
	Autumn	Gd hght of water; open ther, little wind and un, tht leaves; plenty of water, plenty of salmon in the Usk.	Low water, and bright sun shining.	

INDEX

n. refers to note at foot of page.

Adams, Mr. Beale (quoted), 67
Add, the, 45, 219
Alder, 220, 221
Aln, the, 151
America (*see* also Canada), Notes from, 14, 15
Ard, Loch, 183
Ardennes, the, 45, 224
Argyllshire, 46
Armathwaite, 5, 200
Assynt, Loch, 74
Australia, 193, 196
Avon, the Wiltshire, 162
Awe, Little Loch, 214, 220
Awe, the, 25, 46, 234

Bagot, Mr. R. (quoted), 32, 45, 77, 89, 90, 156, 183, 211
Bairnsfather, Lieut. - Col. P. R. (quoted), 22, 98, 133, 182
Baker, Dr. H. B. (quoted), 115, 152, 186, 192, 195, 197, 218, 232
Ballyshannon Bridge, 194
Bandon, the, 8, 61, 77, 128, 143, 158, 172, 180, 214, 234
Banffshire, 85, 190, 216 *n.*
Bann, the, 82, 170

Barbel, 20, 39, 147 (and *n.*), 225
Barker, the Rev. W. (quoted), 32, 90, 167, 215
Barle, the, 13
Barrington, Mr. C. G., C.B. (quoted), 95, 114, 143, 191, 232, 234
Bass, 35, 36, 47, 70, 123, 173, 239
Beane, the, 180
Beechey, the late Canon (quoted), 82, 120, 180, 218
Bell, Dr. Joseph (quoted), 233
Beoraik, Lake, 116
Berwickshire, 118
Bickerdyke, John (quoted), 53-56
Billet, 170 *n.*
Black, Mr. A. W. (quoted), 87, 112, 147, 192, 197
Blackadder, the, 45, 118, 221
Black Forest, the, 45, 223
Blackness of water, 66
Blackwater, the, 213, 221
Bleak, 19, 184
Border streams, 136, 151
Botany Bay, 193
Boulton, Major (quoted), 14, 43, 86, 192

Breadalbane, the Marquess of (quoted), 130, 162
Bream, 41, 85, 99, 148, 168, 240
Bride, the, 99
Bridge, the late Lady (quoted), 95, 141, 159, 188
Bright, Dr. (quoted), 9, 20, 37, 113
Brixham, 43, 173
Broadfoot, Colonel (quoted), 151
Brooke, Sir Douglas (quoted), 86, 147, 153, 222
Brooke, the Rev. J. M. S. (quoted), 6
Brown, Sir G. T. (quoted), 74, 153, 184, 222
Brown, Mr. (late Secretary of the Loch Lomond Angling Association), 56
Brown, Mr. J. (quoted), 71
Bryden, Mr. H. A. (quoted), 97, 116, 170, 224, 226
Buckinghamshire, 84
Budleigh Salterton, 151
Bulkeley, Sir R. (quoted), 135
Burkitt, Prof. F. C. (quoted), 74, 101, 214, 220
Buxton, the Right Hon. Sydney (quoted), 19, 44, 107, 134, 169, 178, 179 n., 181 n., 191, 198, 203, 216 n.

Caldwell, Colonel (quoted), 85, 114, 124, 144, 180, 195, 234
Canada, Notes from, 8, 66, 161, 213
Cantlie, Mr. James (quoted), 85, 115, 190, 216 n.

Carmarthenshire, 86, 119, 185
Carp, 85, 99, 168, 186
Chalk streams, 14
Chambers, Mr. C. E. S. (quoted), 196
Champneys, Mr. Basil (quoted), 40, 46, 159, 160, 175, 176, 177, 204, 208, 229
Char, 98, 170
Charlton, 220
Cheadle, Dr. (quoted), 217
Chess, the, 84
Chetham (quoted), 172
Chree, Dr. C. (quoted), 78, 84
Chub, 39, 55, 147, 148, 167
Climate, the British, 23, 24, 25, 242
Cloonaghmore, the, 185
Clouds, 82, 107, 109, 234
Coalfish, 170 n.
Coarse fish, 55, 148, 149, 175, 241
Cod, 158, 170 n.
Cold weather, 19, 140-150
Coleridge, the Hon. G. (quoted), 45, 68, 80, 114, 162, 188, 209, 234
Coley, the, 13
Collingwood, Col. (quoted), 199, 234
Coln, the, 84, 138, 188
Colne, the, 241
Colour of water, 121-123
Conger, 89 n., 186
Conn, Lough, 192
Connemara, 185
Conner, Mr. H. D. (quoted), 8, 61, 77, 128, 143, 158, 180, 214, 234
Coquet, the, 154
Corbet, Major-General A. D. (quoted), 89

Corwen, 154
Craigover Pool, 80
Creedy, the, 195, 197
Crinan, 219
Cumberland, 136

Dalgleish, Sir W. O. (quoted), 85, 147, 185, 192, 195, 197, 214
Dalton, Major-General J. C. (quoted), 66, 74, 114, 143, 161, 189, 215
Dartmoor, 123, 132, 229
Davies-Cooke, Colonel Bryan (quoted), 27, 28, 50, 122, 170, 188, 220, 232
Dawkins, the late Sir Clinton (quoted), 85, 186, 213
Dawkins, Professor W. Boyd (quoted), 52
Deane, Colonel (quoted), 23, 48, 115, 134, 163, 166, 212, 221
Dee, the Aberdeenshire, 9, 46, 85, 96, 114, 180, 195, 234
Dee (Merionethshire), 153, 185
Derbyshire, 40, 161
Desborough, Lord (quoted), 41, 169, 170 n.
Deveron, the, 188
Devonshire, 13, 35, 46, 110, 193, 197, 229
Devorgana, Lake, 116
Discoloration of water, 108, 121
Discomfort of bad weather, 103, 165, 173, 206, 242
Dodd, Mr. G. A. (quoted), 45, 78, 95, 111, 156, 184, 223, 233
Don, the, 138, 151, 204
Donegal, Co., 86, 115, 147, 186, 192, 197, 235

Downstream wind, 176, 181, 195
Drought, 91, 98
Dry-fly, 107, 110, 134, 169, 176, 178, 182, 229
Dulverton, 104
Dunn, the late Matthias, 29
Dunne, Captain J. J. (quoted), 84, 192

Eamont, the, 136
Earthquakes, influence of, 17, 50
Eastern counties, 96, 172, 180, 182, 193, 195
East wind, 11, 42, 43, 53, 172-189, 190, 196, 197, 204
East-north-east wind, 186
East-south-east wind, 197
Eclipse, possible effect of solar, 34, 35
Eddystone, fishing near the, 47, 239
Eden, the, 5, 58, 200, 202
Edgworth - Johnstone, Captain (quoted), 86, 115, 147, 186, 192, 195, 197, 235
Edinburgh, 87, 137, 147, 192, 196
Edwards, Mr. C. E. Munro (quoted), 25, 76, 88, 93, 115, 126, 135, 146, 184, 199, 215
Edwards - Moss, Sir John (quoted), 50, 77, 99, 113, 124, 142, 209, 233
Eel, 31, 45, 46, 215
Erne, the Irish, 15, 45, 45, 58, 194, 211
Esk, the, 137
Esmonde, Sir T. G. (quoted), 82, 115, 172, 236
Etive, Loch, 60

Exe, the, 13, 104, 151, 192, 216 n.
Exmoor, 132
Eyelids absent in fish, 70
Eyton, Major J. Wynn (quoted), 27, 61, 98, 99, 186, 231

Failure, weather as an excuse for, 3
Fairford, 138, 188
February Red, 99
Ferguson - Davie, Sir J. D. (quoted), 195, 197
Fergusson, the Rt. Hon. Sir James (quoted), 82, 113, 124, 214, 235
Fermanagh, Co., 153
Fetherstonhaugh, Mr. Godfrey (quoted), 185
Fewn, Loch, 101
Field, the, 106
Filey Brigg, 170 n.
Float-fishing, 41, 46, 167, 240
Floods, 37, 38, 108, 124-132
Florida, 41
Fly, colour of the, 21
Foakes-Jackson, the Rev. F. (quoted), 59
Fog, 46, 107, 228-242
Forfarshire, 78
Fowey, the, 186, 193, 198, 236
Fowler, Mr. W. W. (quoted), 86, 119, 185
Francis Francis, story of the late, 56, 57
Frost, 39, 141-150, 204, 235
Funchal, 72

Gallichan, Mr. W. M. (quoted), 40, 45, 85, 96, 98, 120, 145, 154, 161, 224, 230, 232, 235, 240

Gathorne - Hardy, the Hon. A. E. (quoted), 33, 48, 77, 234
Gawthorne, Mr. E. W. (quoted), 162
Gibraltar, 174
Girlsta, Loch of, 84
Gladhouse Reservoir, 137
Gloucestershire, 153
Godley, Major H. C. (quoted), 185, 191, 218
Godwin-Austen, Lieut.-Col. H. H. (quoted), 98
Gomm, Mr. T. W. (quoted), 155
Goola Lake, 185
Gorey, 82
Graeme, Mr. A. M. S. (quoted), 84, 92, 120, 189, 197, 206
Granby, the Marquess of (quoted), 119, 143, 190, 197, 218, 232
Grayling, 28, 39, 54, 74, 78, 85, 104, 105, 106, 122, 145, 150, 161, 168, 185, 189, 226, 239, 240
Gudgeon, 55, 169
Gut, conspicuousness of, 10, 21, 36, 54, 87, 113

Haddingtonshire, 154, 180, 236
Hail, 11, 37, 100, 107, 132-139, 219
Hall, Mr. Hubert (quoted), 30, 31, 44, 97, 181, 193, 207
Hampshire, 14
Hardanger Fjord, 225
Hardy, Mr. J. J. (quoted), 151, 152
Hare's Ear, 99
Harvie-Brown, Mr. J. A. (quoted), 24, 25, 195

Hatch of fly, wind and the, 177
Hatchery, Notes from a, 27
Hawkesbury, the, 193
Heat, 90
Hebrides, the, 44, 86, 167, 192
"Helm" wind, a, 199-200
Helmsdale, the, 12
Herring, 29
Hoar-frost, 144
Hodgson, Mr. W. Earl (quoted), 16, 66, 67, 112, 144, 151, 171, 182, 216 (and n.), 230
Hollins, Miss Rotha (quoted), 199-202
Hot weather, 97
Hunting, frost' and, 3
Hutchinson, Mr. Horace (quoted), 6, 111

Inchnadamph, 214
India, Notes from, 22, 23, 91, 98, 134, 213
Inverness-shire, 116
Ireland, Notes from, 9, 15, 43, 89, 96, 158
Italian fishermen, 71
Itchen, the, 46, 168, 171, 178, 215, 217, 234, 240

Jock Scott, 138

Kaiser Wilhelm Canal, the, 208
Kennedy, Admiral Sir W. R. (quoted), 170, 232
Kennet, the, 134
Kent, the, 77, 89
Kerry, Co., 116
Kingsley, Charles (quoted), 174
Kirkaig, the, 195
Kuram, the, 163

Lake district, the, 200
Lake fishing, 46, 48, 67, 85, 93, 115, 116, 117, 159, 166, 167, 171, 183
Lapland, Notes from, 114, 152, 186, 192, 195, 197, 218, 232
Lazonby, 200
Leinster, Province of, 127, 144
Lethbridge, Sir Roper (quoted), 132
Level of the water, 108, 124-132, 162
Leven, Loch, 42, 86, 116, 118, 172, 180, 183, 195, 196
Lewes, the, 86
Liffey, the, 159
Light, 65-90, 109
Lightning, 205-227
Liver, the, 60
Loch Leven trout, 87, 112, 147
Lomond, Loch, 56, 94

M'Inroy, Colonel Charles (quoted), 43, 122, 123, 156, 191
Mackerel, 41, 71, 72
Madeira, 71
Mahseer, 22, 23, 37, 91, 98, 133, 162, 163
Malcolm, Colonel (quoted), 45, 49, 219
Malmesbury, 220
Man, Isle of, 52
March Brown, 12, 83, 99, 135, 136, 153, 201
Marston, Mr. R. B. (quoted), 46, 145, 240
Mathews, the Rev. W. A. (quoted), 52
Matthews, Mr. A. R. (quoted), 148, 149, 241

Mawddach, the, 126, 127
Maxwell, the Rt. Hon. Sir
    Herbert (quoted), 9, 12,
    36, 70, 80, 142
Mayfly, 79, 97, 180, 220
Mayo, Co., 115, 185
Mediterranean, torch-fishing
    in the, 71
Melbourne, 174
Meoble Forest, the, 116
Merionethshire, 93, 154, 184
Mertoun, 80
Mevagissey, 29
Michelmore, Mr. H. (quoted),
    13, 38, 110-111
Minchin, Mr. C. O. (quoted),
    35, 158, 186
Minneapolis, 83
Minnow-fishing, 76, 184
Mist, 46, 228-242
Mold, 27
Montagu of Beaulieu, Lord
    (quoted), 11, 131, 138
Montagu, Sir S. (quoted),
    171, 215, 234
Moore, Colonel St. Leger
    (quoted), 6, 45, 127,
    144, 157, 159, 188, 210,
    225
Morgan, Mr. J. Lloyd
    (quoted), 203
Morton, Major-General Sir
    G. de Courcy (quoted),
    23, 33, 133, 134, 162
Moss-water, 122
Murray, Dr. G. (quoted),
    154
Murray, Dr. W. (quoted), 5,
    154

Namsen, the, 90
Naver, the, 50
Ness, the, 8
New South Wales, 193
Noble, Mr. Robert (quoted),
    45, 118, 137, 154, 180,
    221, 236
Noe, the, 60
Norfolk, Notes from, 30, 31,
    44, 97, 207, 240
"Normal weather" theory,
    Colonel Bairnsfather's,
    22, 23, 98, 182
North, the Rt. Hon. Sir Ford
    (quoted), 45, 46, 211,
    237
North-east wind, 43, 44,
    136, 153, 174, 180, 185,
    188, 189, 190, 191, 198,
    217
North Esk, the, 123, 156,
    191
North Tyne, the, 45, 77,
    211
Northumberland, 45, 77, 120,
    154, 219
North wind, 43, 53, 183,
    189-193
North-west wind, 190, 192,
    204
Norway, Notes from, 9, 46,
    66, 90, 96, 97, 114, 152,
    161, 174, 184, 186, 192,
    195, 197, 218, 224, 226,
    232

O'Callaghan, Major-General
    Desmond (quoted), 45,
    78, 120, 122, 191, 219
O'Grady, the Hon. F. Stan-
    dish (quoted), 6
Olive Duns, 26
Orchy, the, 25, 130
Orkney, 84, 92, 120, 188,
    197, 206
Otter, the, 151, 184, 192,
    216 n.
Oxidation of the water, 10,
    37

Peal, 88 *n.*

Peat stain, 121, 122, 126

Pennines, the, 200

Penton Hook, 156

Perch, 41, 55, 74, 85, 147, 148, 168, 239

Perthshire, 78, 94

Pike, 54, 55, 97, 148, 149, 162, 167, 174, 239

Pilchard, 29

Piscatorial Society, the, 241

Pollack, 41, 186

Portuguese fishermen, 71

Pottinger, Sir Henry (quoted), 75, 124, 125, 139, 174, 226

Rain, 11, 37, 107-132

Rainbow-trout, 83, 185, 191

Rajawrie Tawi, 98

Rashleigh, Sir Colman B. (quoted), 186, 193, 198, 236

Rising short, 33

Rising water, 124-131

Ristagouche, 8, 213

Roach, 20, 39, 41, 46, 55, 100, 147, 148, 149, 161, 162, 168, 169, 226, 240, 241

Robson, Mr. Mayo, 60

Rockies, fishing in the, 15

Rolt, Mr. H. A. (quoted), 28, 39, 76, 100, 146, 148, 161, 168, 169, 189, 226, 239, 240, 241

Ross-shire, 60, 81, 114

Russell, Major-General J. C. (quoted), 234

Russell, Mr. W. (quoted), 56, 86, 94, 138, 178 *n.*, 181 *n.*, 218

Sadler, Mr. W. Dendy (quoted), 67

Salisbury, 162

Salmon, 9, 28, 36, 39, 42, 45, 50, 53, 57, 58, 68, 69, 73, 77, 80, 81, 85, 86, 88, 95, 96, 99, 113, 114, 124-129, 131, 135, 141, 142, 143, 144, 145, 146, 147, 150, 156-158, 159, 167, 174, 183, 184, 185, 187, 188, 191, 192, 194, 195, 197, 209, 220, 221, 233, 234, 236-238

Sand River, the, 78, 184

Schnapper fishing, 193

Scotland, Notes from, 8, 9, 12, 13, 14, 33, 40, 42, 67, 85, 160, 178 *n.*, 185, 213, 233

Sea-bream, 71

Sea-fishing, 43, 47, 51-53, 55, 71, 158, 173, 189, 193, 196, 197, 238

Sea-trout, 9, 11, 32, 39, 54, 60, 77, 86, 88 *n.*, 89, 131, 138, 167, 171, 188, 209, 215, 233, 234

Senior, Mr. W. (quoted), 104-106, 146

Seton-Karr, Sir H. (quoted), 8, 9, 14, 32, 48, 58, 83, 96, 129, 194

Sewin (*see* also Sea-trout), 88, 126, 146, 184, 215

Seymour, Admiral Sir Michael Culme (quoted), 5

"Shade-fishing," 75

Sheild, Mr. A. Marmaduke (quoted), 82, 113, 116-118, 125, 128, 135, 183, 231

Sheringham, Mr. H. T. (quoted), 17, 41, 50, 74, 85, 90, 100, 119, 133, 146, 148, 167, 185, 197, 239, 241

Shetland, 84, 85, 138, 216 n.
Shooting, rain and, 3
Shrimp, fishing with, 74, 143
Sight in fishes, 20, 36, 66
"Silver Doctor," 50
Skaig, 74
Skating, importance of temperature in, 4
Sky reflections, 67
Slaney, the, 45, 157, 187, 210
Sleet (see Hail)
Smart, Mr. J. E. (quoted), 151, 184 216 n.
Snow, 11, 39, 58, 100, 107, 150-158
"Snow-broth," 39, 68, 158-163, 204
South wind, 44, 175, 189, 196-199
South-east wind, 50, 197
"Southerly Buster," 196
South-south-west wind, 198
South-west wind, 53, 147, 167, 178, 179, 195, 197-199
Spanish fishermen, 71
Spates, 37, 126
Spean, the, 159
Spey, the, 46, 211, 212, 237
Spring fishing, 25
Stead, Colonel (quoted), 163
Stewart, W. C., 67
Stewart tackle, 132
Stour (Suffolk), 149
Stroud, 153
Suffolk, 149
Suffolk and Berkshire, the Earl of (quoted), 138, 204, 219
Sunset, effects of, 32, 88-90
Sunshine, (see also Light, Hot weather), 11, 31, 58, 74, 75, 77, 78, 142, 184, 186, 235
Sutherland, 101
Swansea, the Bishop Suffragan of (quoted), 57
Sweden, Notes from, 170, 232
Sydney, 196
Symptoms, 16
Symptoms of weather, Mr. Hodgson on, 66, 216, 230

Talyllyn, Lake, 26, 115
Tarpon, 41
Tawe, the, 86, 119, 214
Tay, Loch, 98, 162, 170
Tay, the, 13, 14, 85, 147, 185, 192, 195, 197
Teign, the, 13, 35, 123, 239
Temperature (see also Cold weather, Hot weather), 19, 161, 177, 195
"Tempests" in Norfolk, 30, 208
Tench, 41, 85, 168, 186
Test, the, 229
Thames, the, 14, 49, 95, 147, 169
Thames trout, 9, 11, 39, 45, 131, 155, 156, 184, 225
The Angler's Vade-Mecum, 172
The Wonderful Trout, 24
Thunder, 11, 35, 44, 205-227
Thunder and lightning, 113
Thurso, the, 9, 95, 96, 142
Till, the, 120
Tingwall, 84
Torbay, 173
Torches in sea-fishing, 71
Torridon, the, 45, 46, 68, 81, 114, 162, 188, 209, 234
Towy, the, 57, 167, 203
Trout (see also Sea-trout,

Thames trout), 11, 12, 13, 14, 15, 16, 19, 23, 26, 27, 28, 30, 32, 36, 39, 42, 44, 45, 48, 54, 57, 61, 74, 75, 78, 82, 83, 84, 86, 87, 88, 89, 92, 93, 94, 95, 96, 97, 98, 99, 100, 106, 110, 111, 112, 113, 114-121, 129, 130, 132, 133, 135, 136-139, 142, 145, 146, 147, 150, 151, 152, 153, 154, 156, 158, 159, 160, 165, 167, 170, 172, 174, 178, 182, 183, 184, 185, 186, 190, 191, 192, 195, 197, 198, 200-202, 207, 215-226, 230, 231, 232, 233, 235, 236, 240, 241

Trout Fishing, 16

Tulla, Loch, 130

Tulloch, Major-General Sir A. (quoted), 8

Tulloch, Mr. J. S. (quoted), 85, 138, 216 n.

Tully, Lake, 185

Tummel, Loch, 116

Tweed, the, 9, 14, 80, 96, 128, 129, 130, 136, 172, 180

Tyne, the (Haddingtonshire), 154, 180, 236

Uist, North, 14

Upstream wind, 170, 176, 181, 197, 198, 199

Usk, the, 8

Wales, Notes from, 14, 26, 27, 40, 57, 126, 127, 146, 161, 215, 230

Walton, Izaak, 175, 196

Wansbeck, the, 45, 219

Warwickshire, 97

Waterford, Co., 99

"Water-smoke," 240

Waterville, 116

Waterways, thunderstorms follow, 208

Weather-lore in animals, 26, 30, 31, 207

Weir-fishing, 184

West, Colonel W. Cornwallis (quoted), 14, 153

West coast, 181, 195

Westmorland, 77, 89

West wind, 44, 53, 147, 170 n., 175, 189, 190, 193-196, 199

Wet-fly, 169, 176, 229, 240

Wey, the, 95, 147

Weybridge, 147 n.

Wheeley, Mr. C. H. (quoted), 11, 19, 45, 49, 95, 100, 131, 147, 148, 156, 162, 184, 186, 215, 225, 234

Whiting, 41, 47

"Wilkinson," 213

Wind (see also East, North, South, West), 40, 164-204

Wolverton, Lord (quoted), 133, 144, 214, 234

Worm-fishing, 74, 75, 78, 126, 161, 190, 225, 230

Writers, limitations of the older, 173, 175, 196

Wylye, the, 168

Wyoming, fishing in Northern, 15

Yellow stain in the water, 122

Yorkshire, 52

Printed by R. & R. CLARK, LIMITED, Edinburgh.

Lightning Source UK Ltd.
Milton Keynes UK
UKHW012158271118
333084UK00008B/301/P